REIKI HAND POSITIONS

A FULL-COLOR PICTORIAL

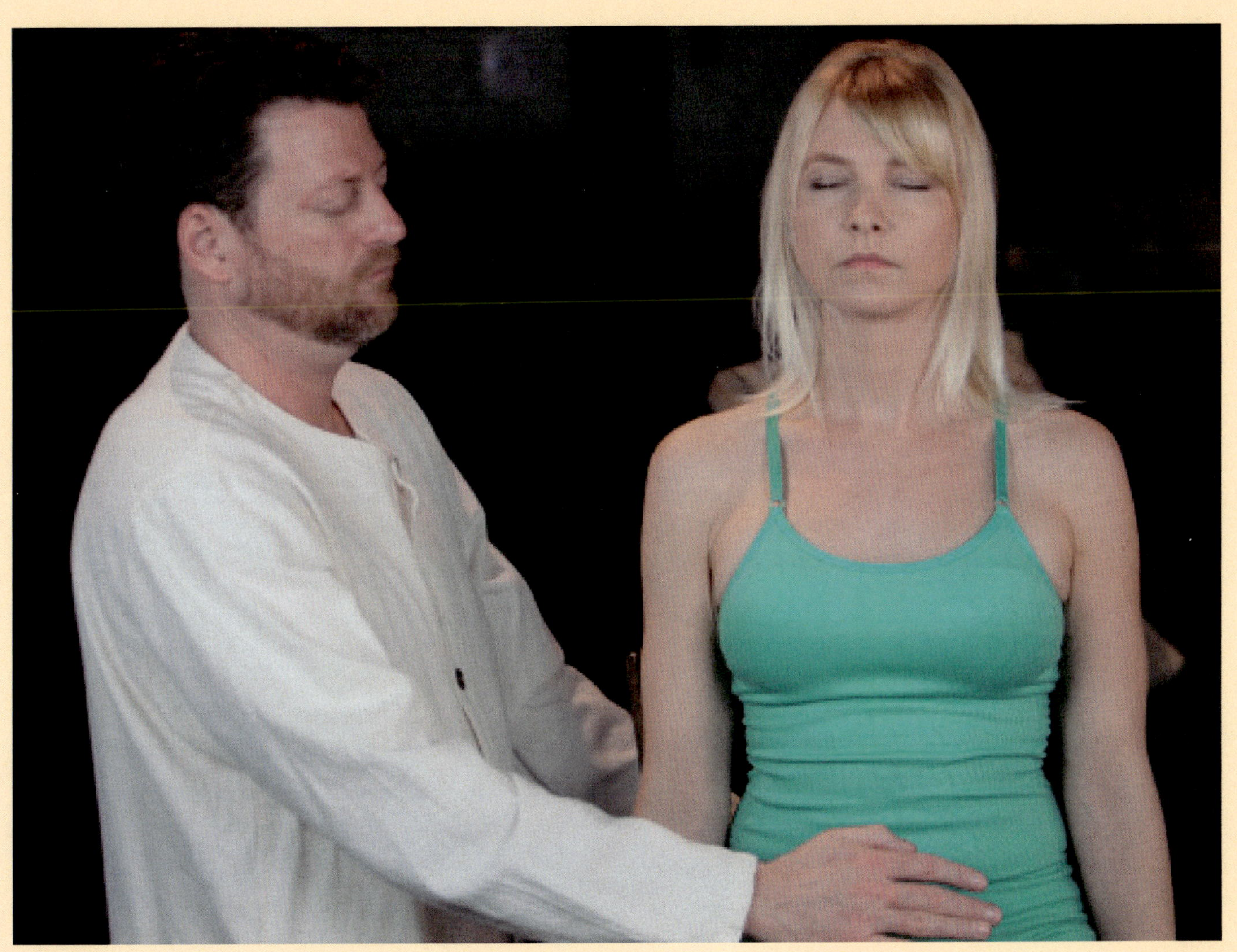

JEFFREY M. DONOVAN

REIKI MASTER TEACHER

I welcome the use of this material for and by other Reiki Master Teachers. However, unlawful or unauthorized use is not permitted. For information on using this book for your classes and/or workshops, please go to: www.HomeStudyReiki.com

ISBN 978-0983469520

Dedicated to healers everywhere and to those healers who came before us, who blazed the trail and showed us the way.

Table of Contents

Author's Message

This book is not intended to replace proper Reiki instruction. It is meant as a study tool to enhance your knowledge of Reiki. There are many good books which can teach you virtually all you need to know to practice Reiki on yourself and others, but there is a critical element you cannot receive from any book, an attunement from a qualified Reiki Master. An attunement is a ceremony which opens your healing channels and tunes your energy field to channel the specific frequency of Reiki. This is what makes Reiki unique from other healing methods. Attunements can be done in person or from a distance.

Many people have told me they've been naturally doing Reiki their whole lives, but didn't know what it was. That's not Reiki. It might be healing, it might be very good healing, but it isn't Reiki. Time and again when these natural healers come to me for 'official training,' they later report that the attunement took their healing ability to a whole new level. Please do not think you can simply emulate the hand positions here in this book and you'll be doing Reiki.

Reiki can be performed hands-on or hands-off, depending on the comfort level of the practitioner and the client. The pictures in this book show the hands-on positions (except where it's not appropriate to touch), but each of these positions can be replicated a few inches off the body.

I've seen many incredible things in my years of practicing Reiki. You'll find amazing stories of physical, spiritual and emotional healing throughout this book. But the stories I've included here are not my own. Instead, I've received testimonials from people all over the world who have had experiences worthy of sharing...some are my students, some are not.

I truly hope you find this book helpful, enriching and/or inspiring. Happy Healing!

Namaste,

In the Summer of 2012, I underwent liver treatment for Hepatitis; a disease that attacks the liver. It mostly consisted of weekly injections and 6 pills daily. Just before I would have to inject myself I felt the trauma, so I would try to the best of my ability to channel Reiki energy to help with the side effects. I have seen people who get extremely ill from liver treatments, but for the most part I was OK! I heard comments from family and friends who knew what was going on, and said that no one would have guessed what I was going through. I don't feel I went through as much pain or just 'feeling sick' as some.

I'm glad it's over and I truly believe Reiki helped a lot with my healing throughout the six month adventure! Now that I'm not on anymore medication, I feel Reiki energy a lot stronger.
~Julie F., Canada

I was hit with a very bad case of pneumonia after my dad passed away. I was in excruciating pain physically and was emotionally drained. With a very high fever, I refused to take more antibiotics. I was intuitively guided to two Master level healers. It was my first time and I had no idea what was going to happen. At around 10:30 pm my pain suddenly stopped! My fever broke and I could actually eat again! I was very shocked and surprised in the best of ways! I knew something had been done to help in my healing. When I checked my email first thing in the morning, it turns out, Lloyd had connected with me at that time! I have had several sessions done after that and am a firm believer in the power of Reiki. Next weekend, I will be graduating from completing Level One Reiki.
~Rohia P., Canada

Healing Yourself

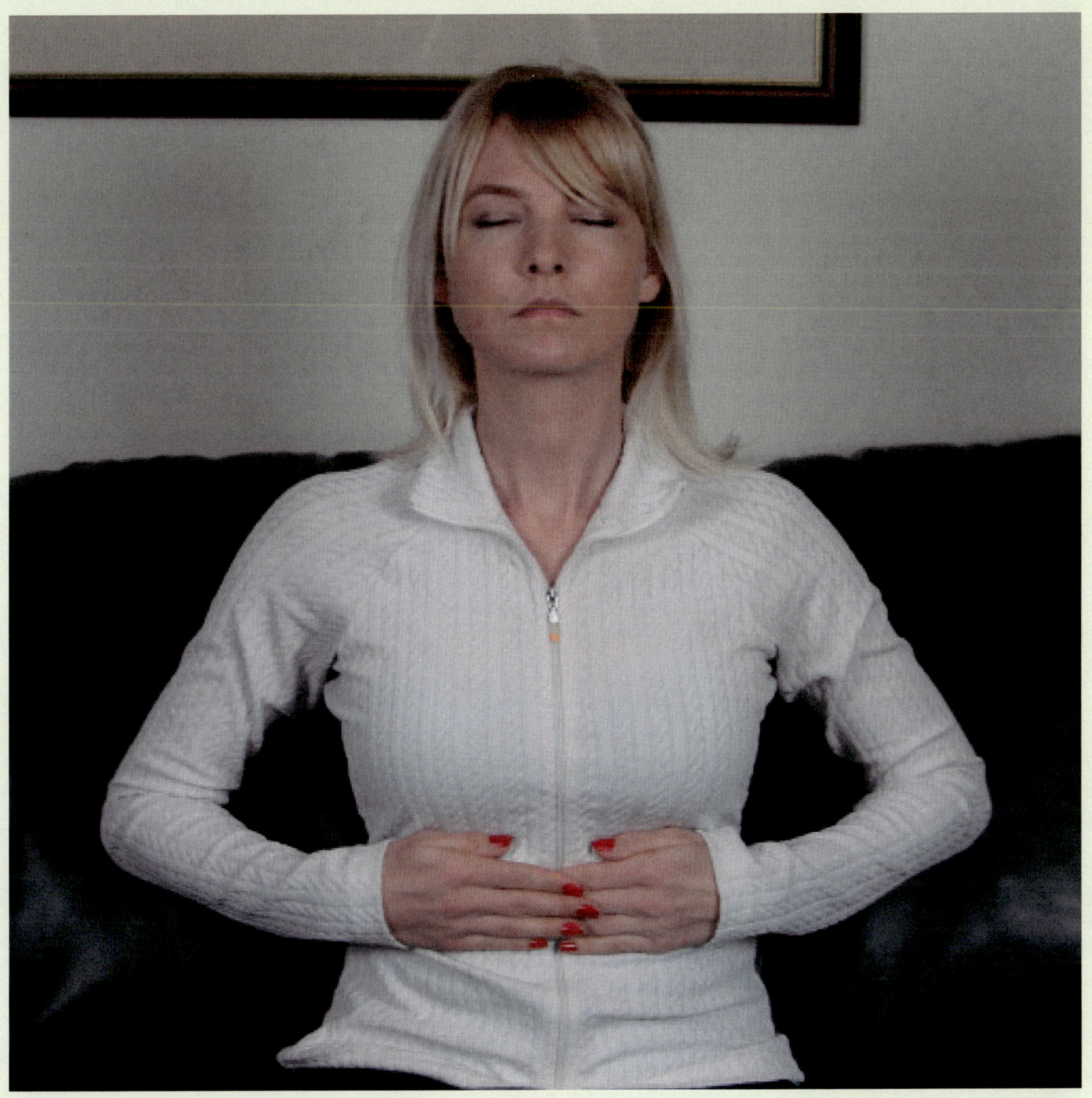

Crown

Head/Neck

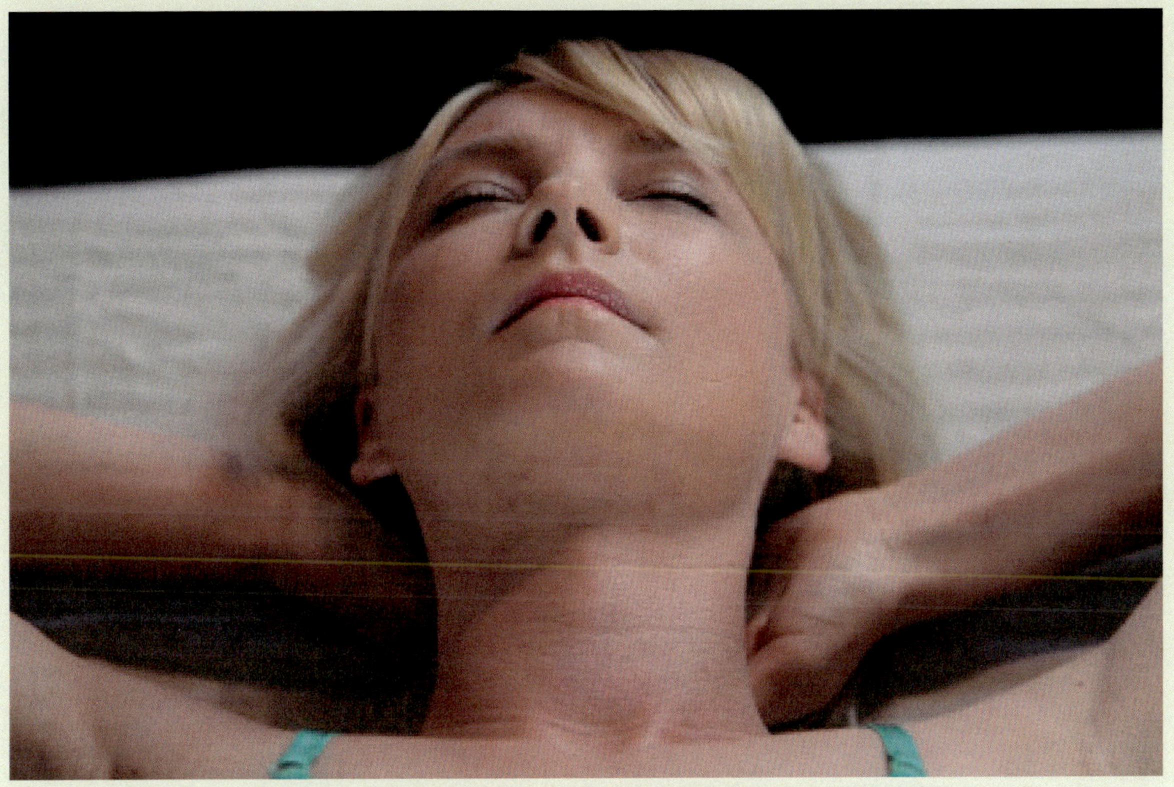

Optional Position - Ears
(Instead of Head/Neck)

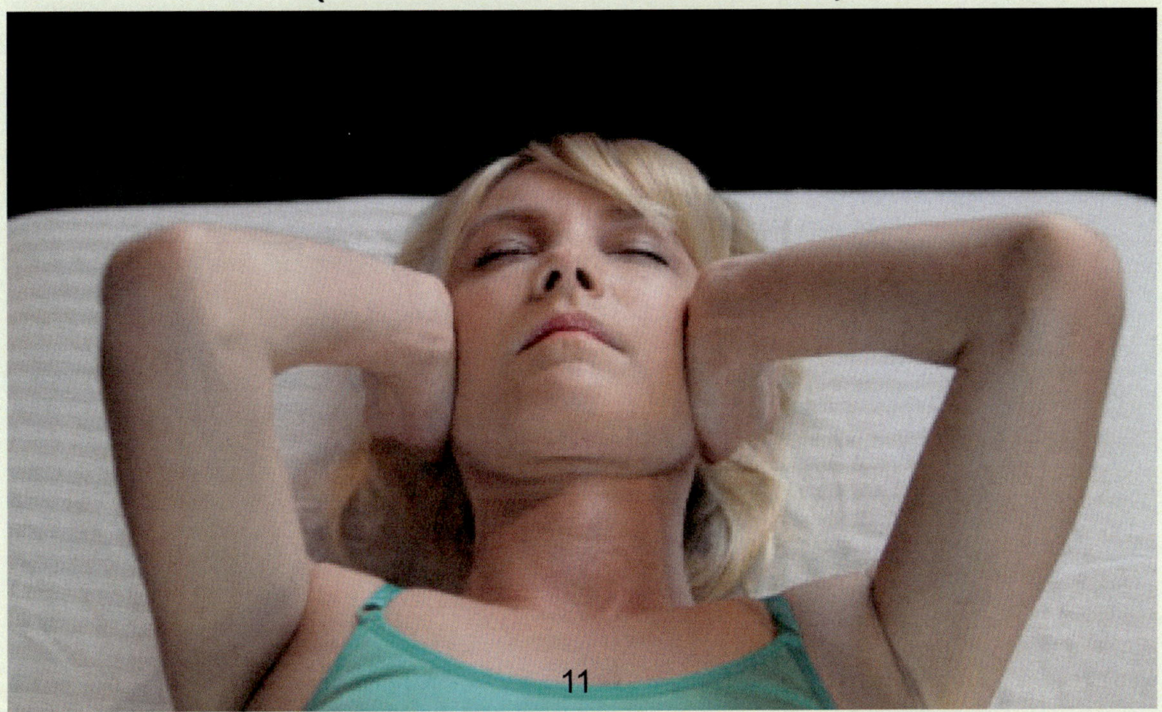

Third Eye

Throat

Throat - Alternate Position

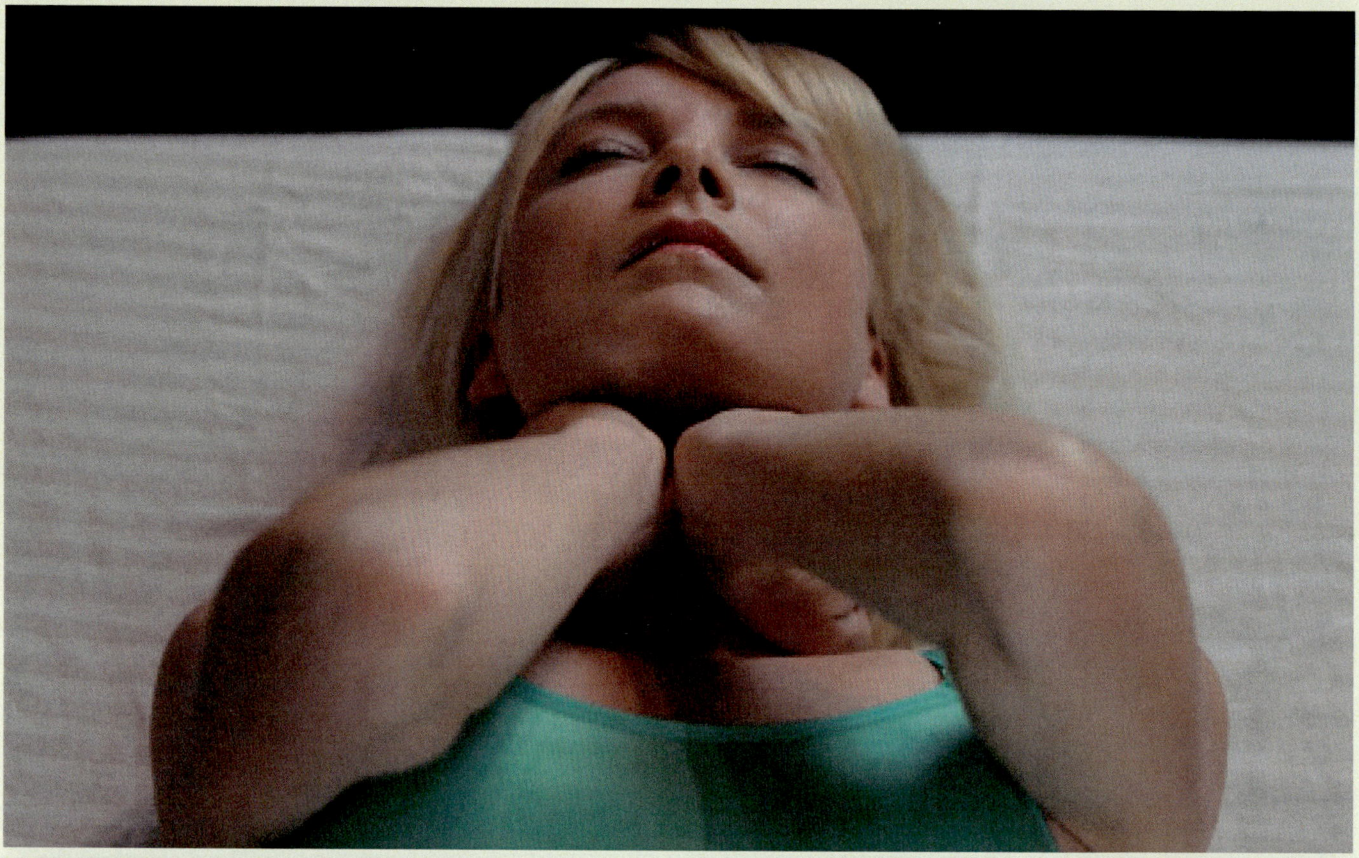

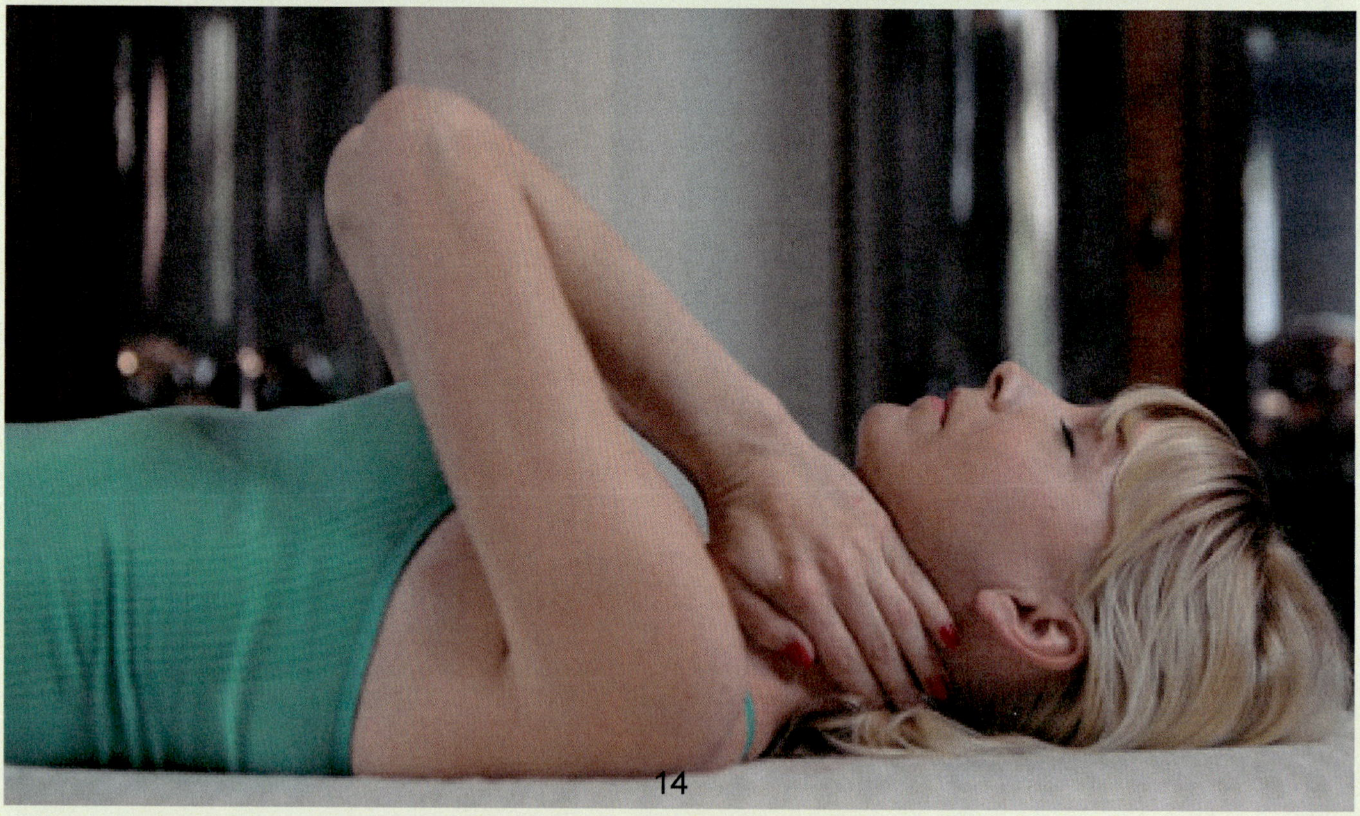

Heart Chakra

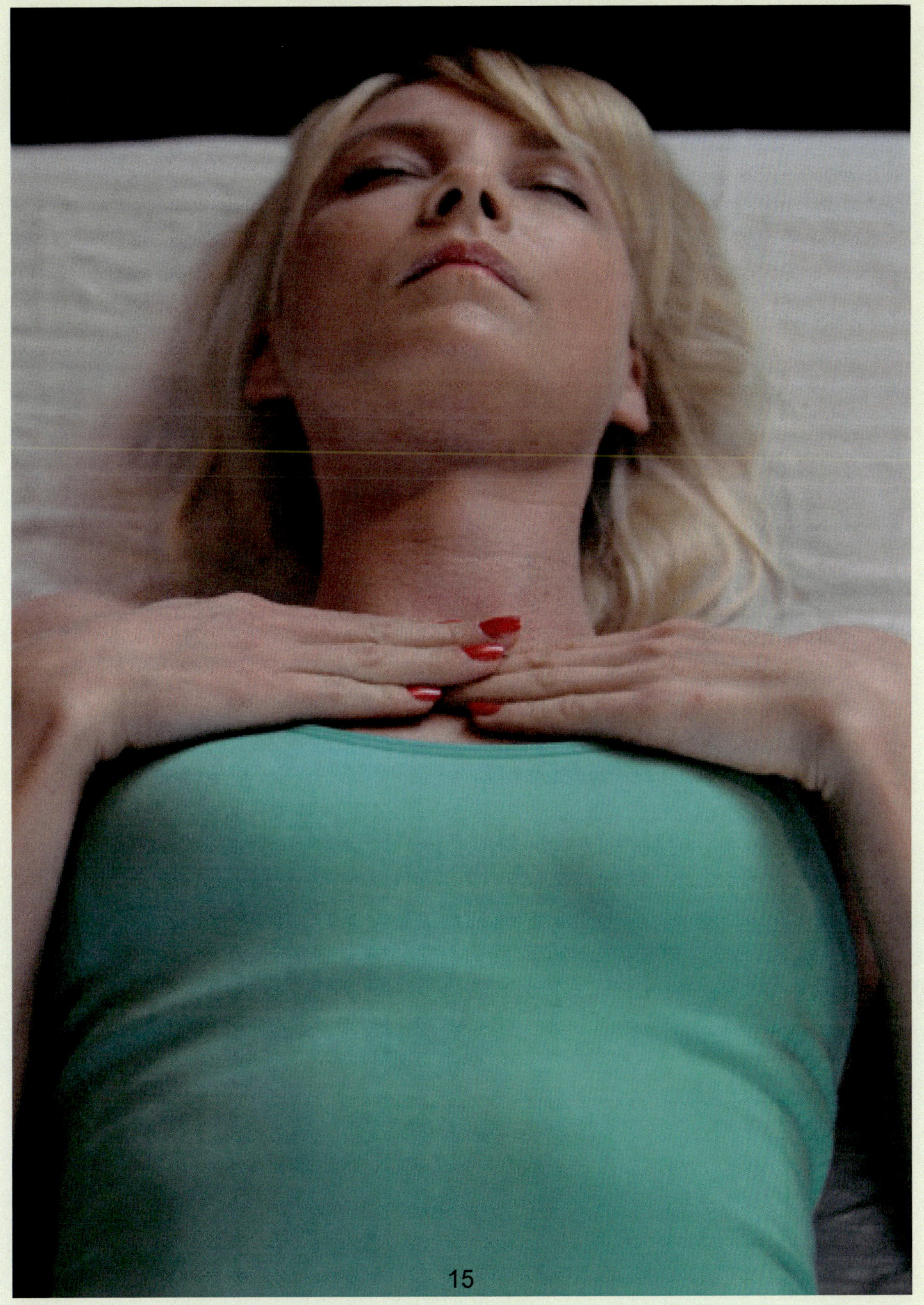

Solar Plexus

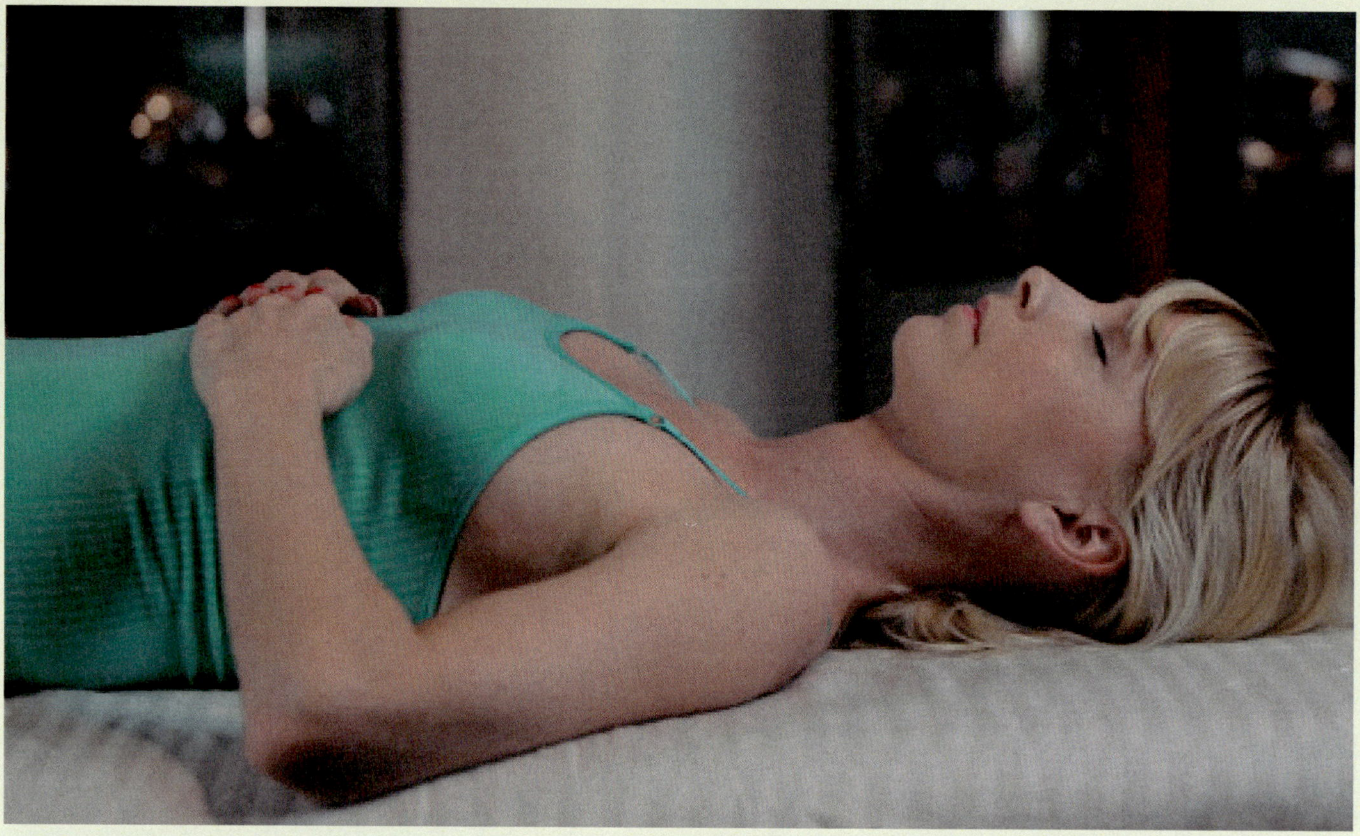

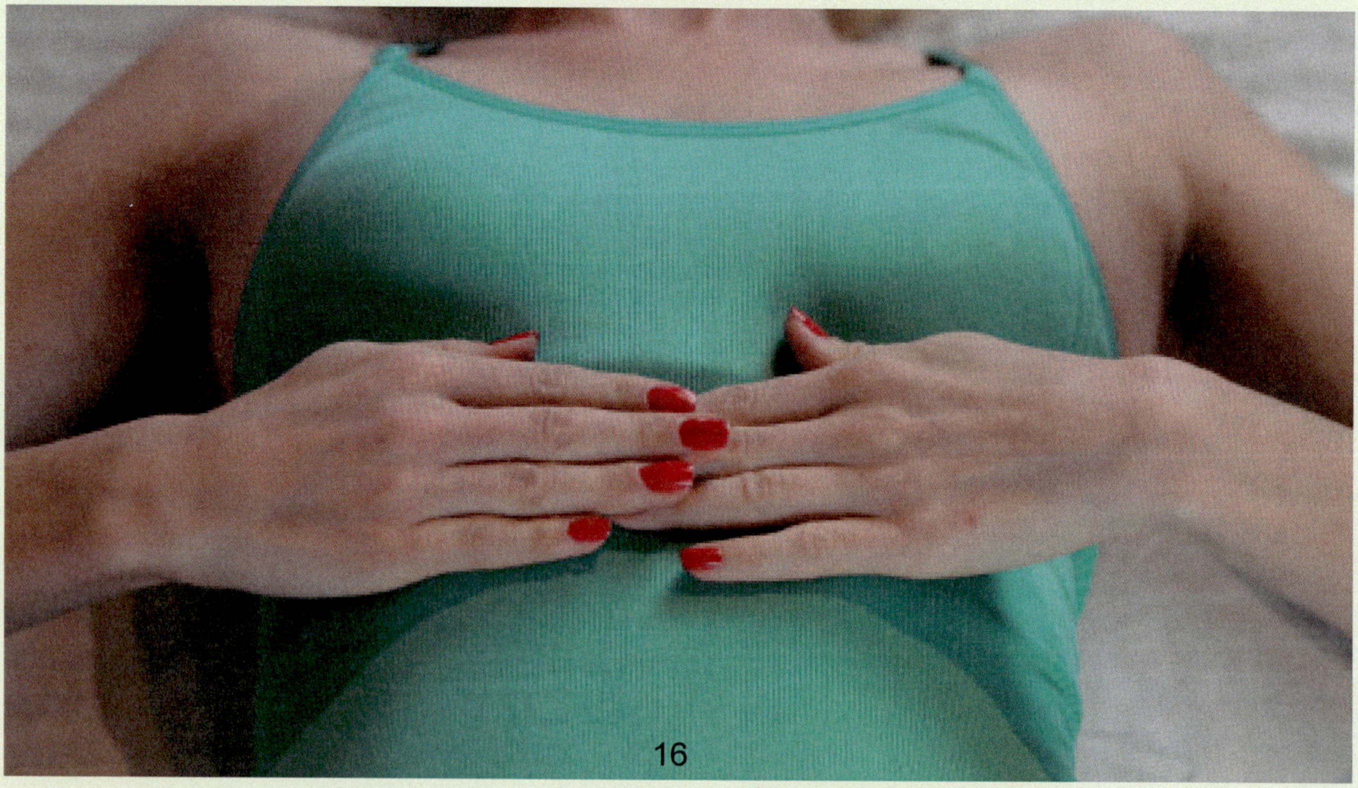

Sacral Plexus

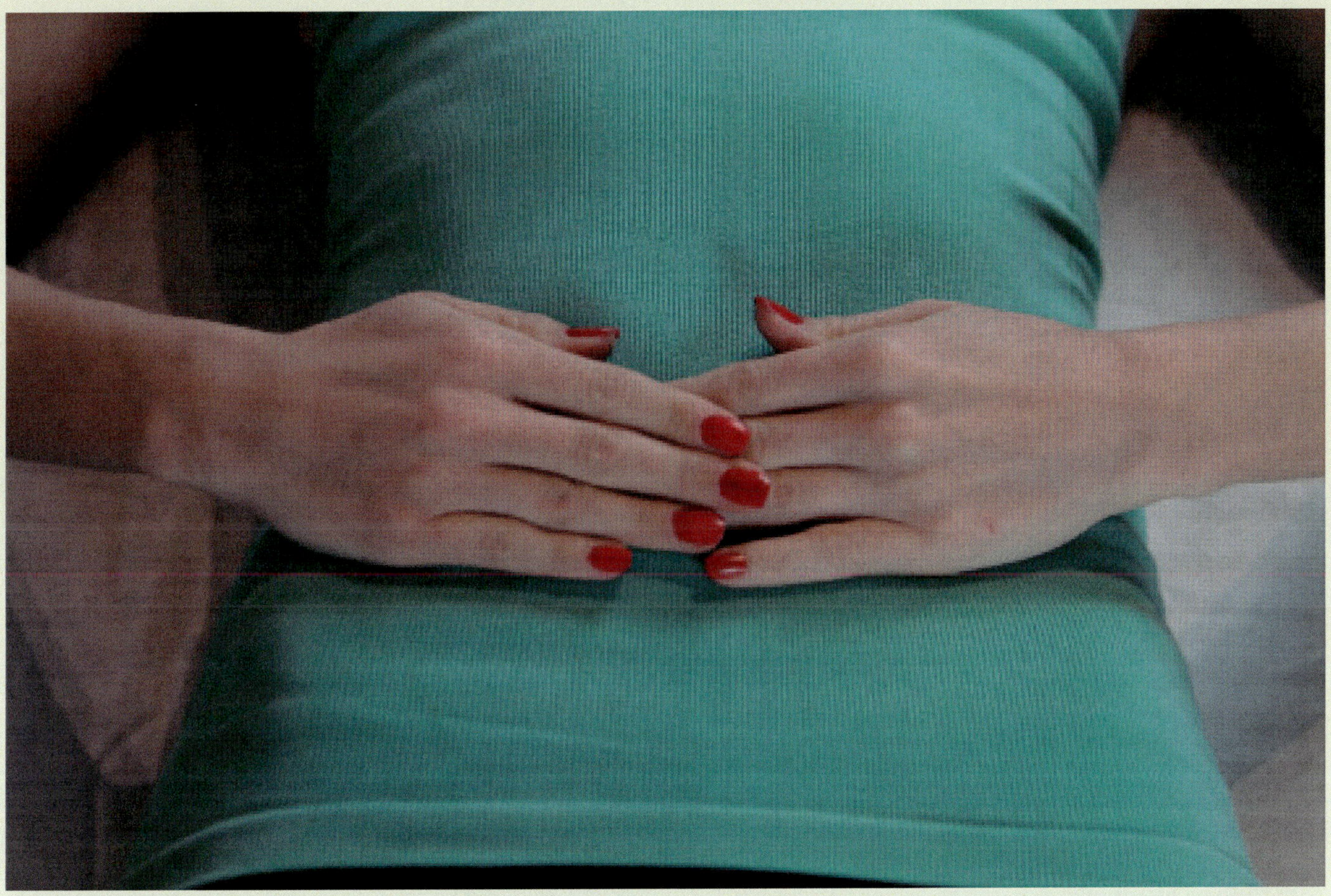

The Sacral Plexus is located near your waistline, just below your belly button.

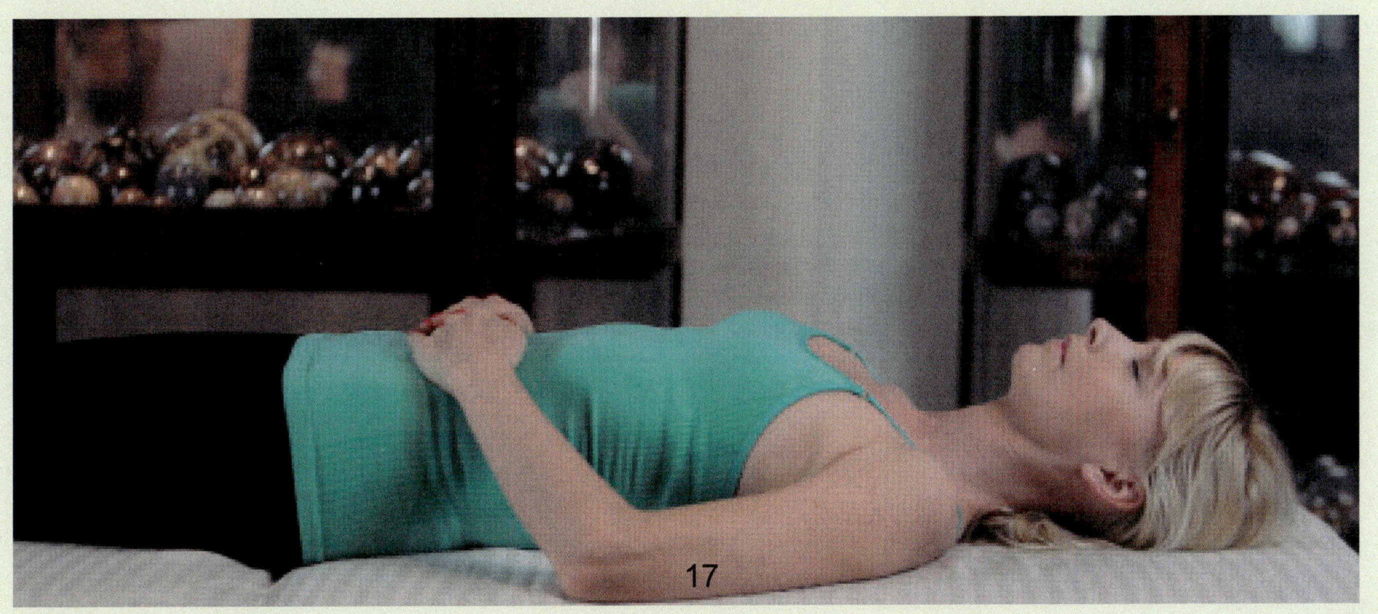

Root Chakra

Cover your genitals

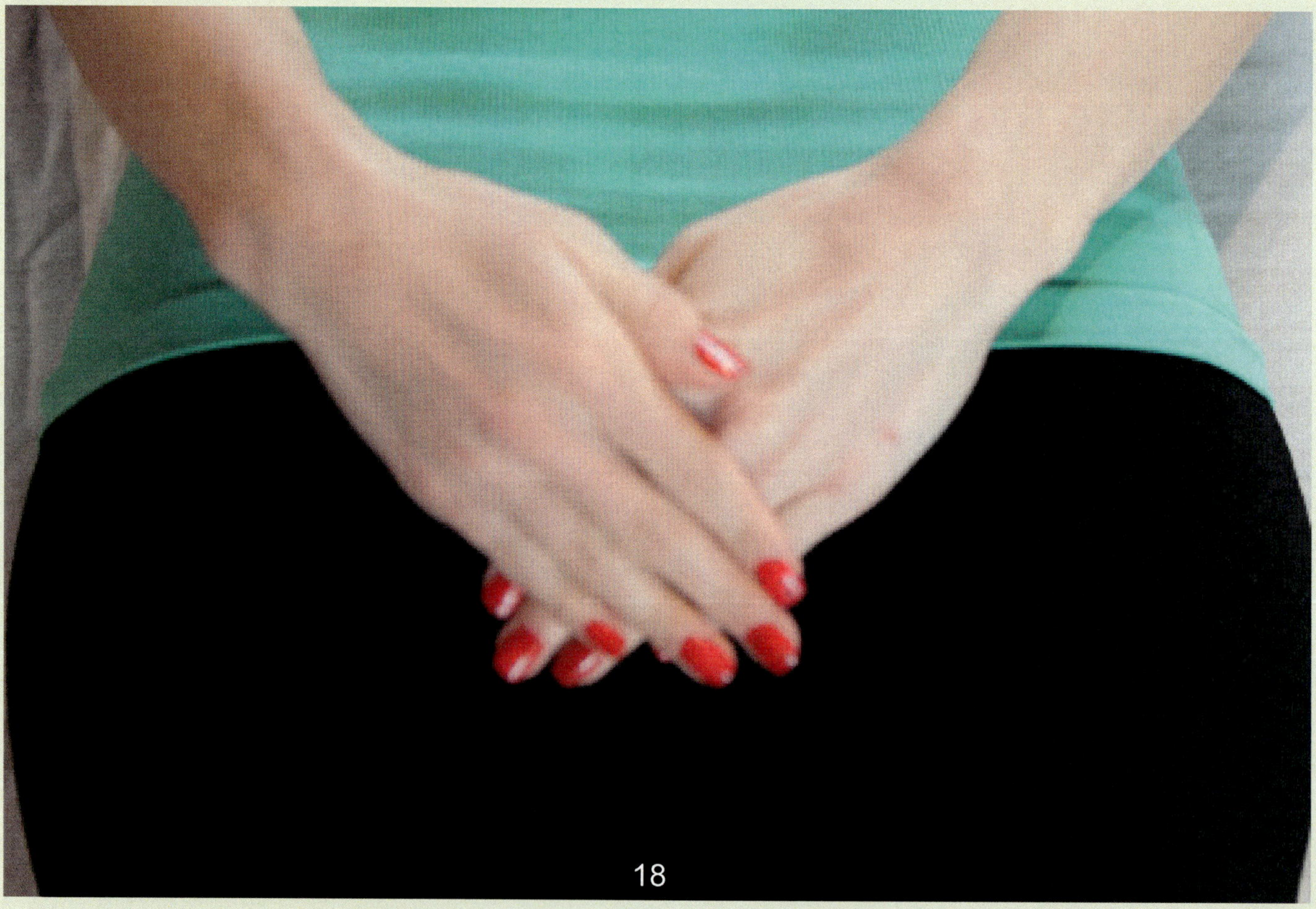

The best thing that has every happened in my Reiki career is the workings on a 5 year-old autistic boy. When I first started working with this child he was non-verbal, screaming out of control all the time and non-compliant. After the first session, the child became happier and more responsive to our world today. I have now been working with this child for 6 months in a Reiki position as well as supporting him with education. He is now talking, reading, speaking in front of his class and following instructions at home and at school. I am amazed each and every time I work with this child at his change. The school has been asking the parents what they have been doing so different to last year. They tell them Reiki.

I love what Reiki does and every day I'm in amazement to what I can offer each and every client.

Love and light,
Paula D., Australia

In the fall of 2008, my six month old grandson was diagnosed with a hernia. His parents decided to take him for a second opinion, upon which the doctor confirmed the presence of the hernia. Surgery was scheduled for the week after Thanksgiving. I spent Saturdays with my grandson during this period of time. Each day we were together, I lovingly placed my hands on his little body. He cooed, kicked and laughed out loud. His parents took him back for his pre-op examination and no evidence of the hernia was found. It left us all speechless at the miraculous power of not only the human body but also the power of Reiki. Surgery was cancelled.
~Besty P., USA

I have been doing Reiki on my (adopted) daughter. She was 18 months old when she came to live with us 5 months ago. She has a hole in her heart and they said she would eventually need surgery. The worst case scenario would require open heart surgery and the very best we could hope for would be laparoscopically through her armpit. The doctor told her previous foster mother that it would NOT heal itself....it just doesn't happen. Today I took her to see the cardiologist and she was amazed. The hole is getting smaller. Now the laparoscopic surgery is the worst case scenario and the hole completely healing itself is the best. She will DEFINITELY NOT need open heart surgery now. I've also been using Reiki on our son (they are twins). He had a blocked tear duct that required surgery. I only did Reiki on him for a couple months before we noticed that his eye had completely cleared. Honestly, I thought it was a complete coincidence until Angel's cardiology appointment yesterday. Now I know that it was not a coincidence at all. I continue to be amazed by the power of Reiki and the human body every day. What a feeling!!
~Denise G., Canada

When I was a freshman in high school, I had severe anemia which caused me to run low on energy before the lunch hour, which was almost halfway through the day; it started to effect not only my grades, but my attitude as well. One day as I entered the classroom, a friend of mine who had studied Reiki, noticed I was nearly about to faint from how exhausted I was. A few moments after I sat down in my chair, I felt an overwhelming amount of energy envelope me and brought me out of the fog. I knew immediately what had happened since I am incredibly sensitive to energy and such. I just looked up and they were looking back, acknowledging that their healing had been received. Each day after that they continued to do so, and it helped me not only get through the day but it helped me get through my anemia. I am completely healthy now and I truly feel without their help, I would still be a grouchy zombie!
~Gina S., USA

Healing Others

Begin With the Shoulders

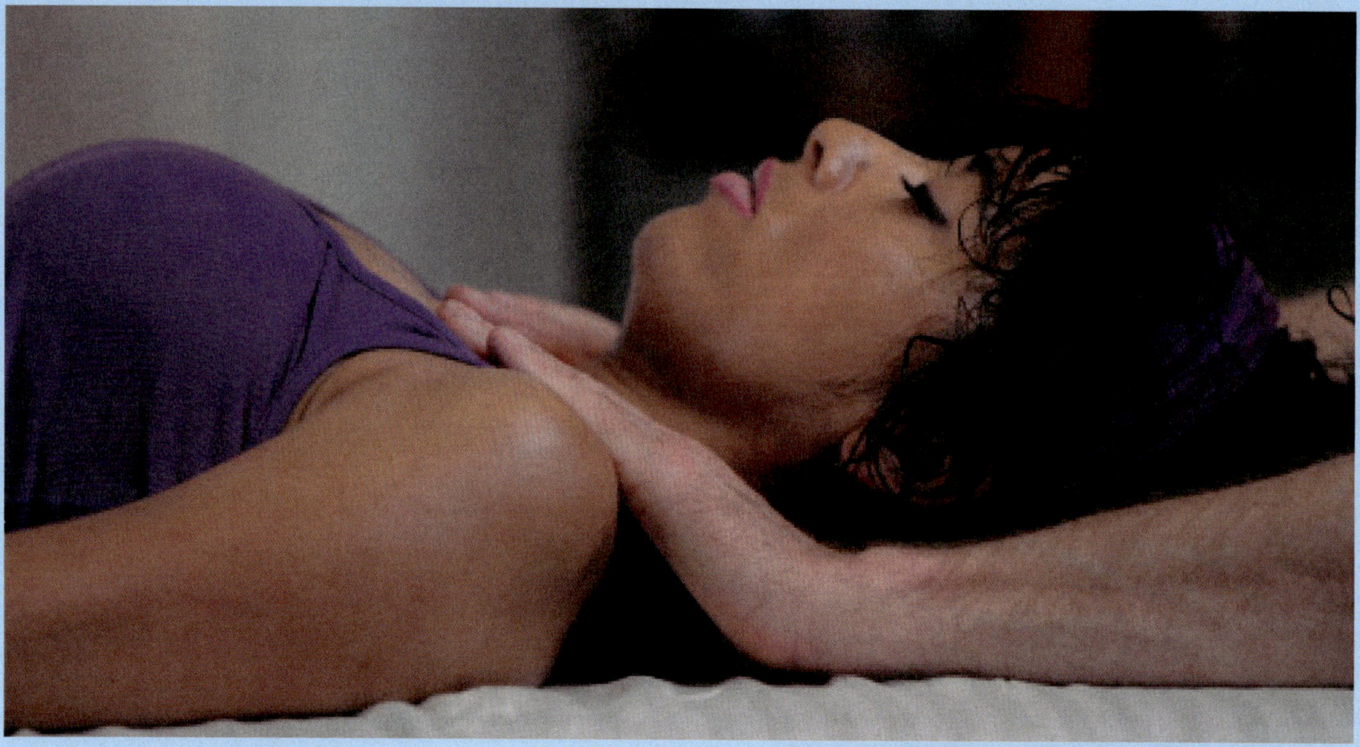

This isn't normally taught as one of the traditional Reiki hand positions, but I like to start a session by placing my hands on the client's shoulders. This helps to establish a connection, give the client a feel for the energy and help to relax the client.

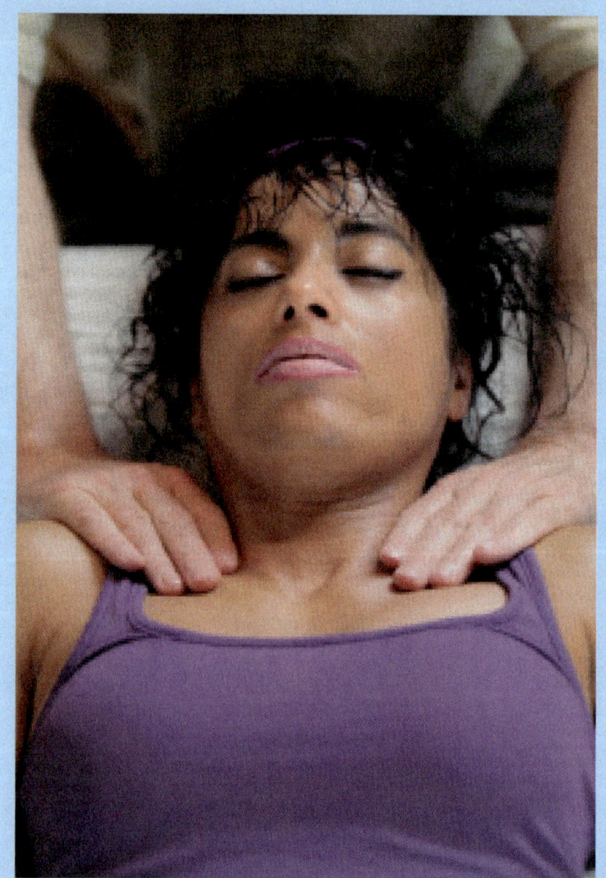

Crown Chakra

Use a very light touch. Reiki is not massage...pressure is not necessary for effective treatment.

Head/Neck

Gently tuck your hands underneath the neck and the back of the head. Some teachers will instruct you to put your hands completely under the head, but the head is heavy, and after a short time, will likely cut off the circulation to your hands and make you uncomfortable, so I prefer to tuck my hands under the head with my fingers under the neck.

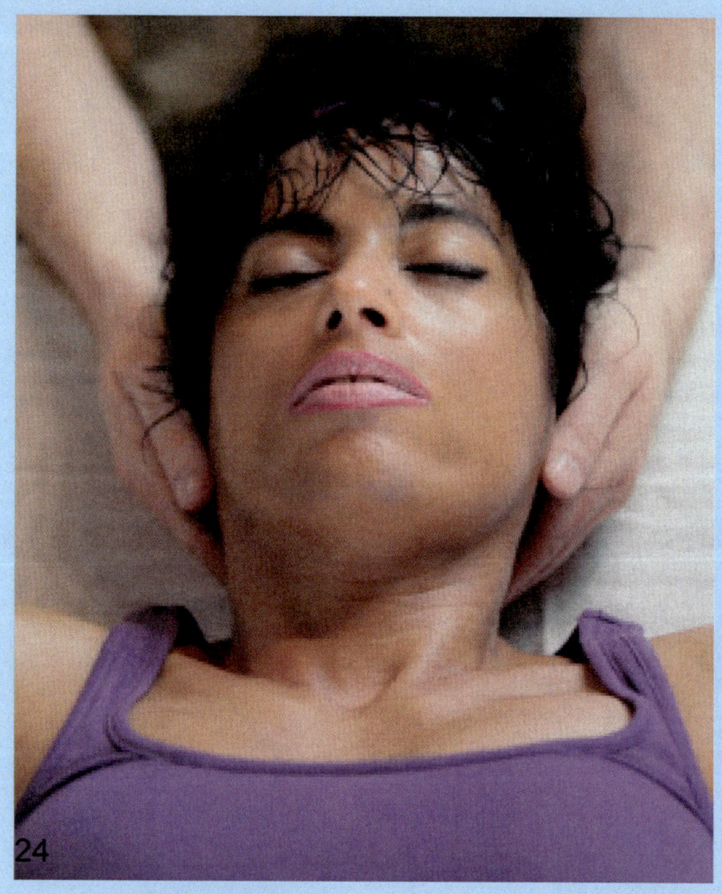

Third Eye

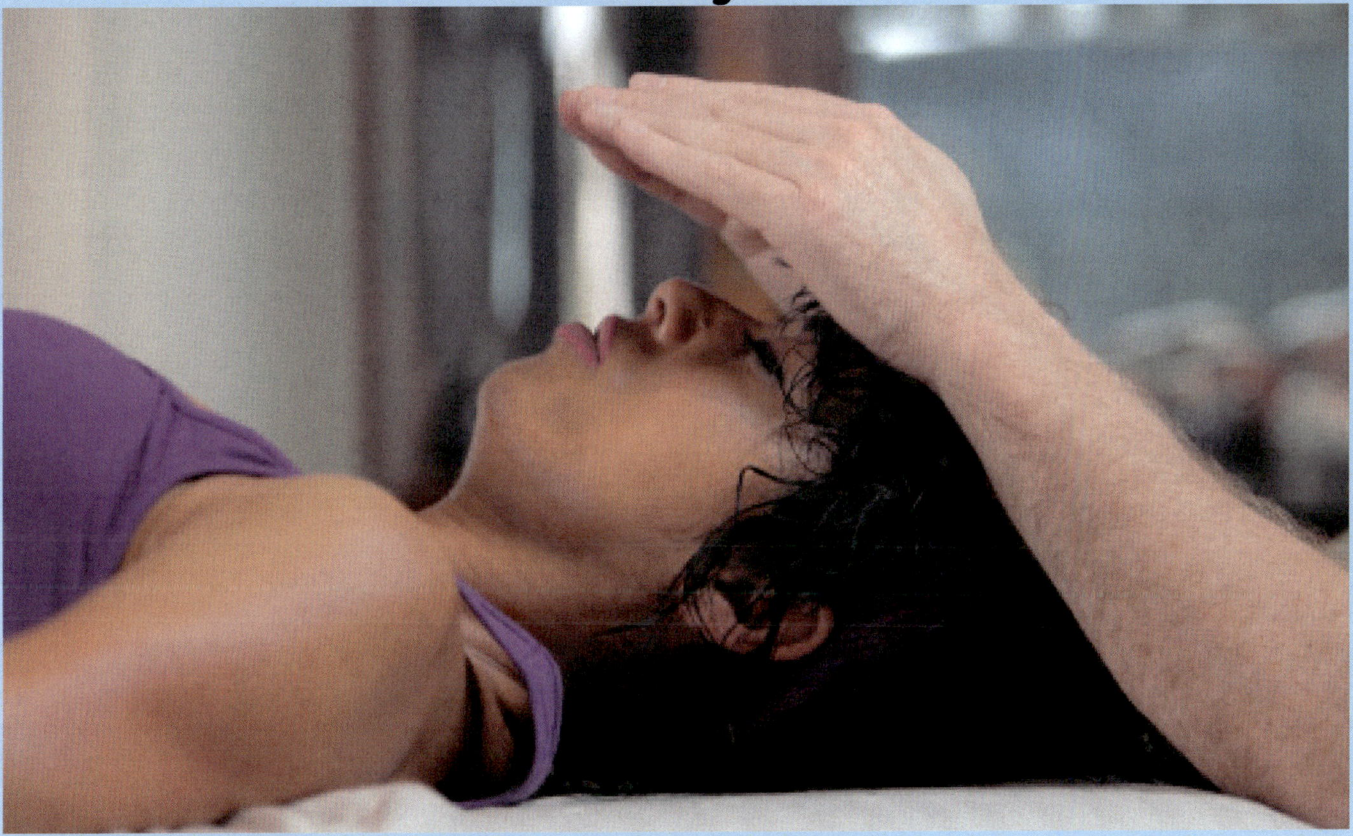

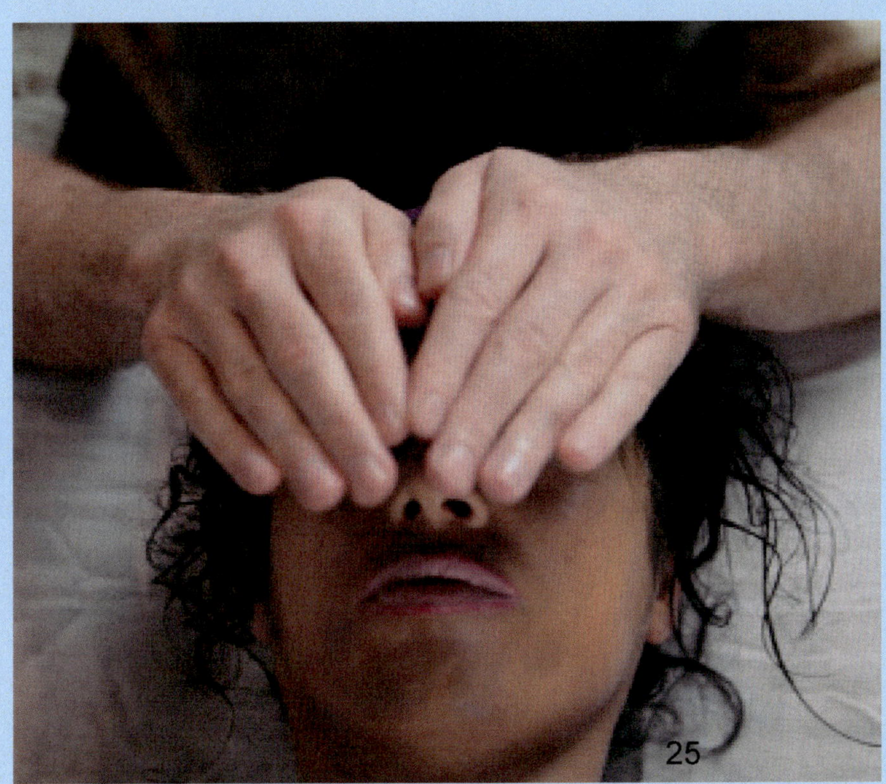

Notice how I leave room for the client to breath freely. You don't want to make the client feel like they're being smothered in any way.

Throat

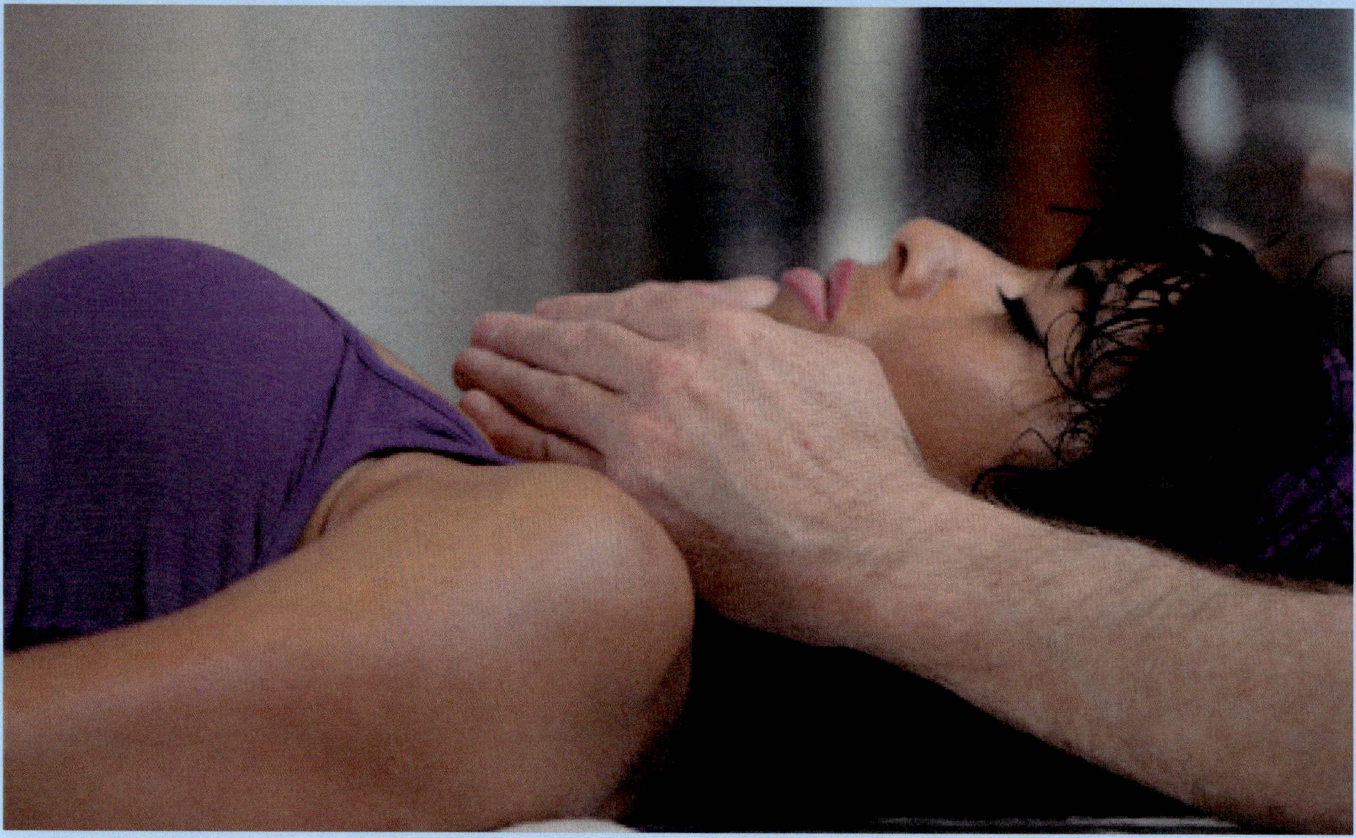

Be gentle when you place your hands over the throat...*GENTLE*. There should be no pressure...You're not choking your client!

Heart Chakra

Solar Plexus

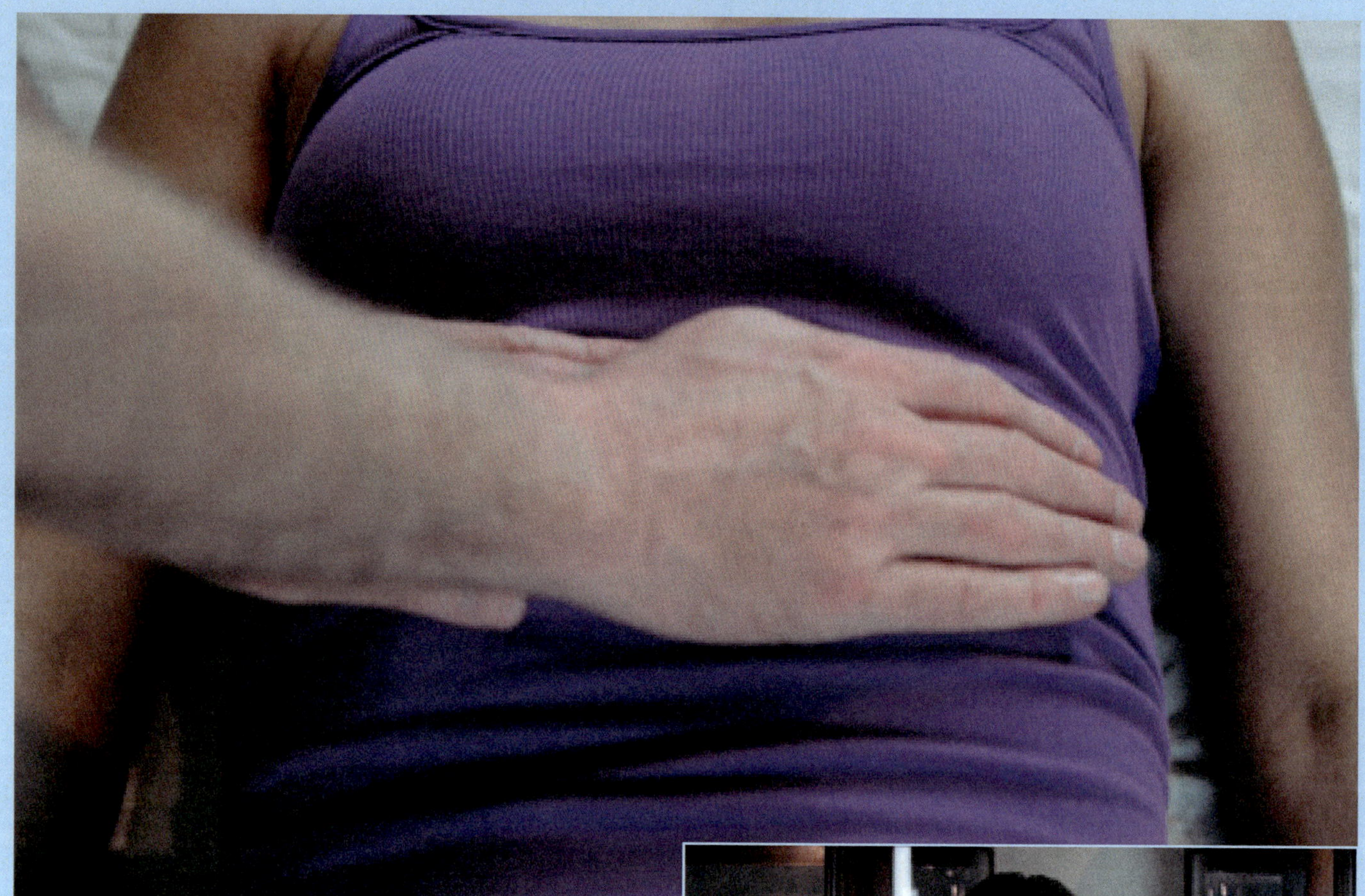

My friends who are at Reiki 3 level saved my life from having cancer of the tonsils...my doctors and surgeon were shocked at my results. They said they were staggering. I can't recommend Reiki enough, it really did save my life.
~Sarah P., United Kingdom

Sacral Plexus

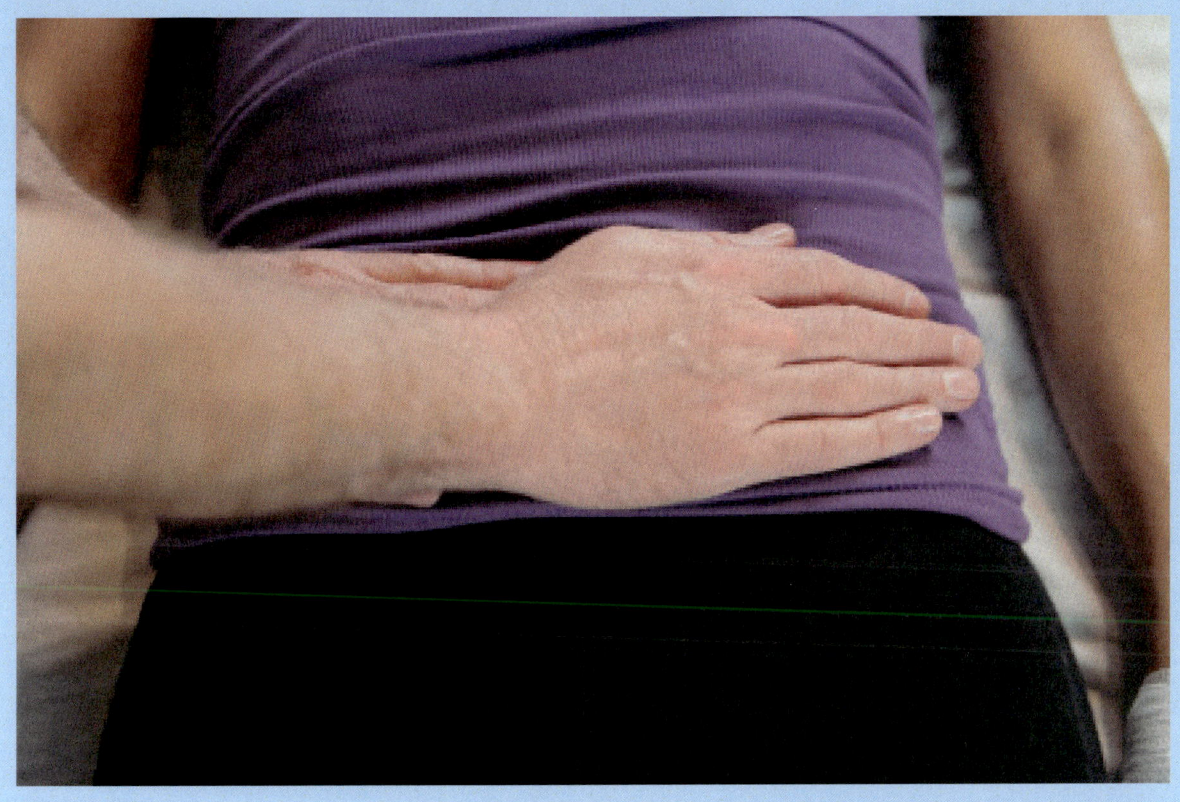

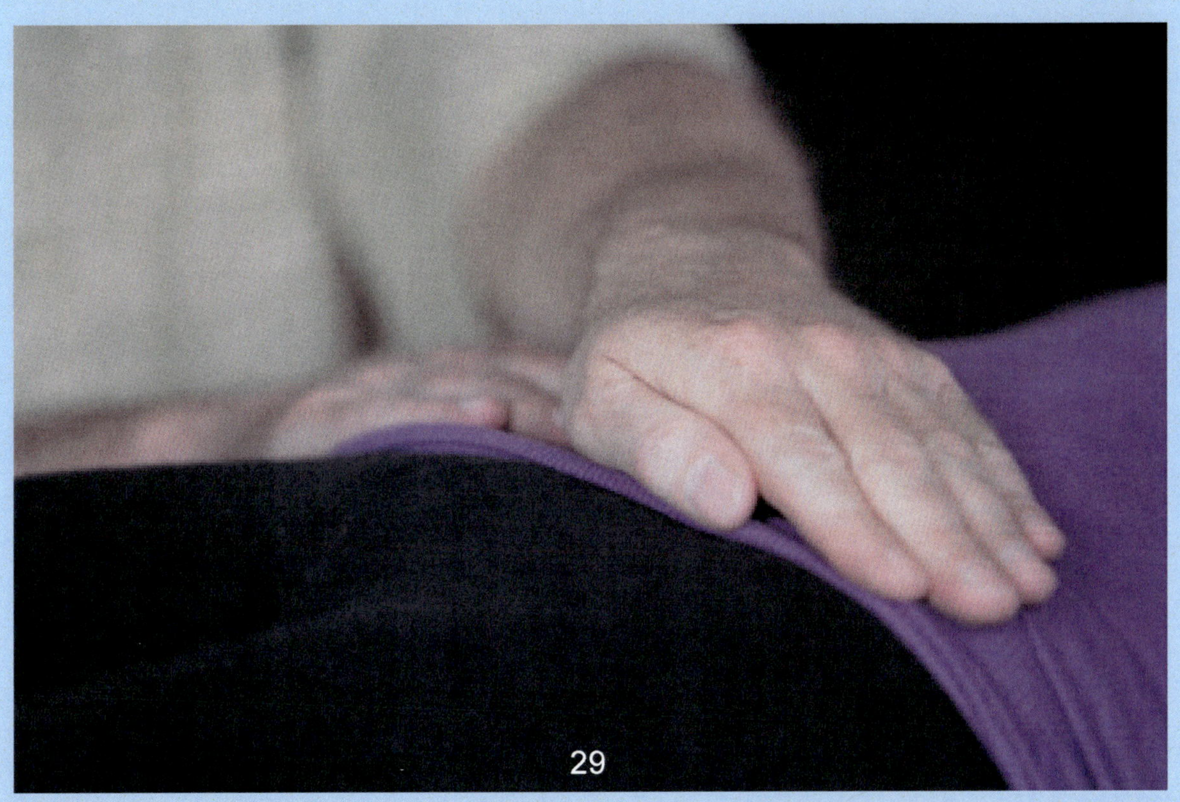

Root Chakra

We never touch the breasts or genitalia. Effective healings can be done without ever touching the body. Keep your hands several inches above the body when appropriate as shown.

Knees & Feet

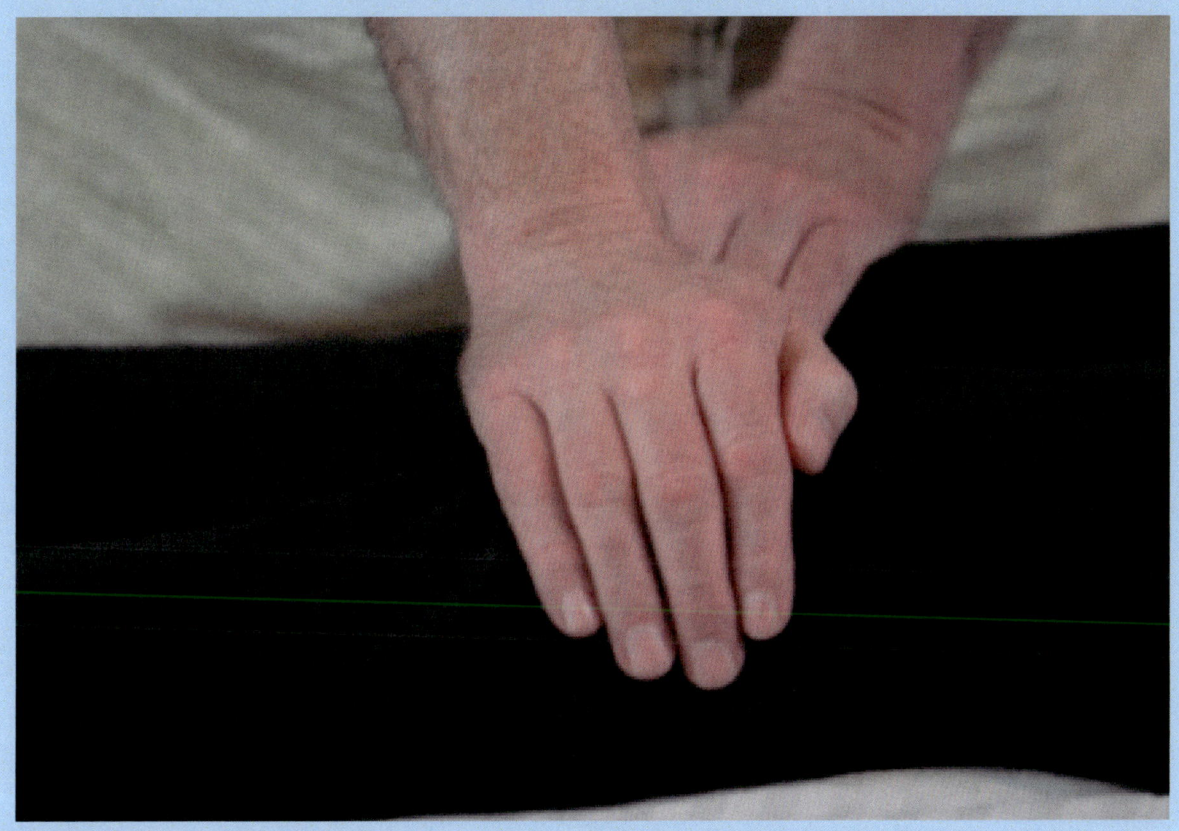

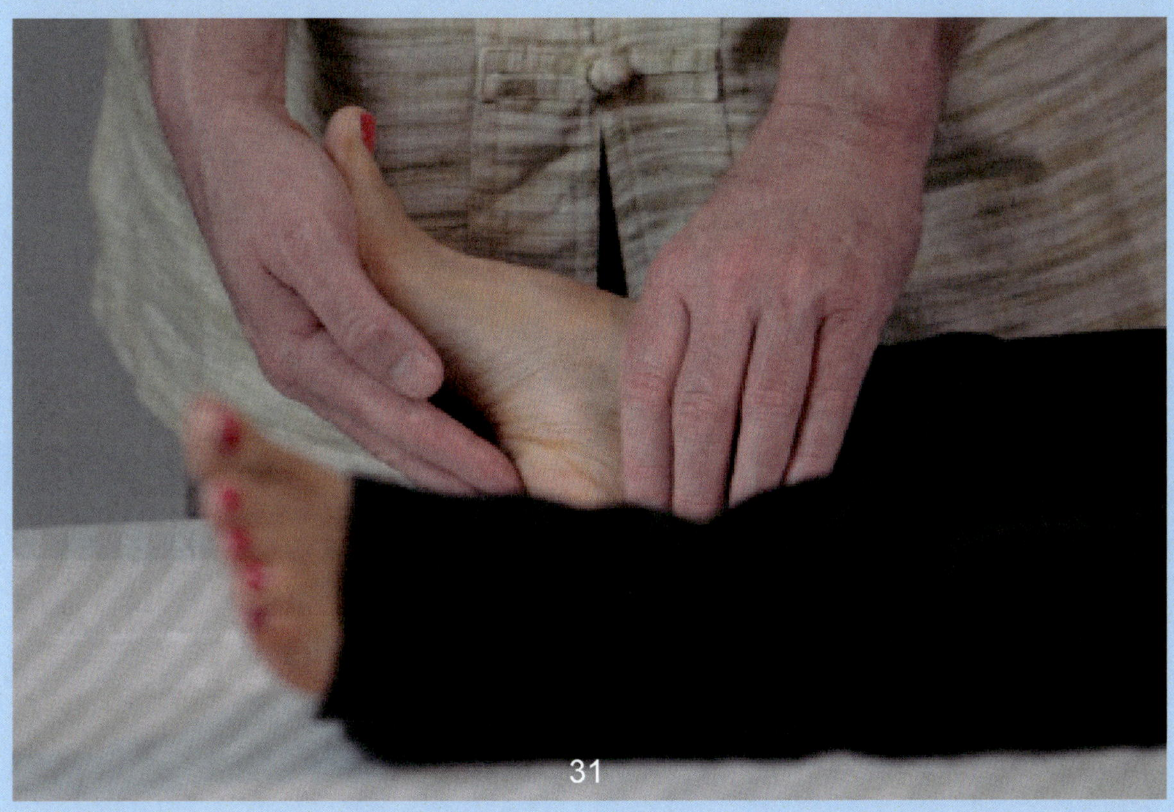

Other Stuff

You can also spread your hands out and allow the energy to flow through your client. Often times after a healing, the client will report waves of energy flowing thru them. I usually will do this in addition to the normal hand positions, not instead of.

Treating Injuries

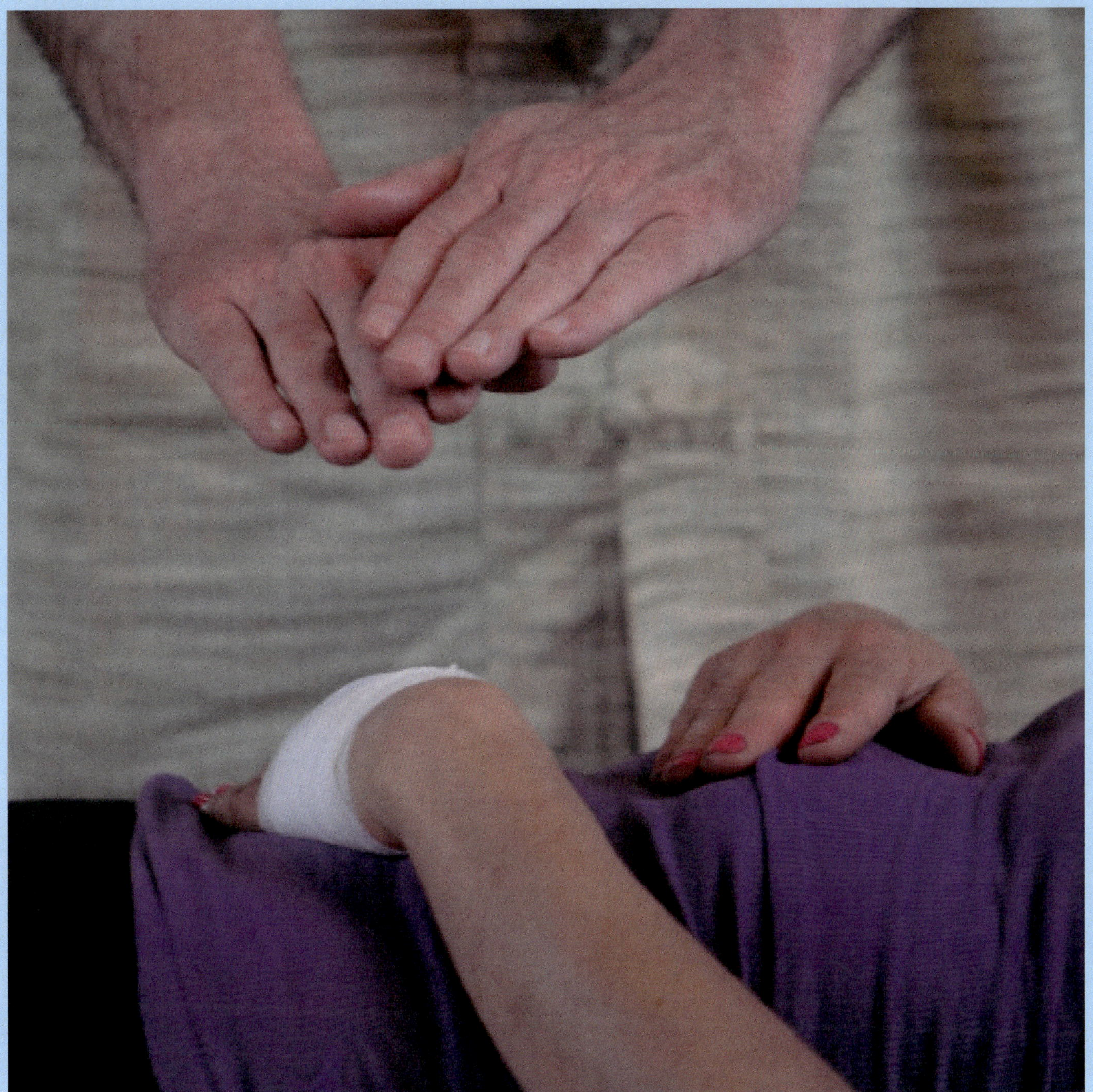

If your client has an injury that would be painful if you touched them, then don't touch. Although touching is not a necessary part of Reiki, most people find the touch relaxing. Each client and situation needs to be evaluated for their specific needs.

Treating the Back

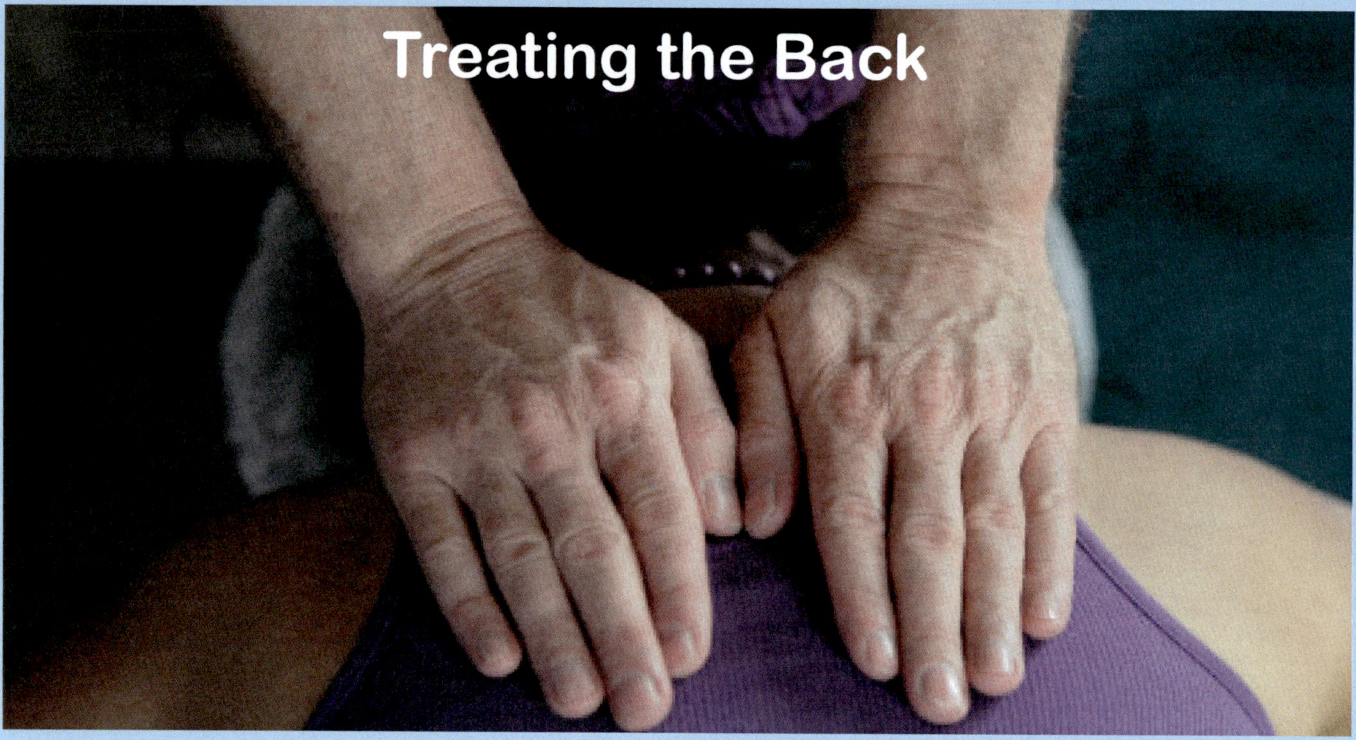

The back positions are more or less the same as the front...all the same chakras are respresented on the backside.

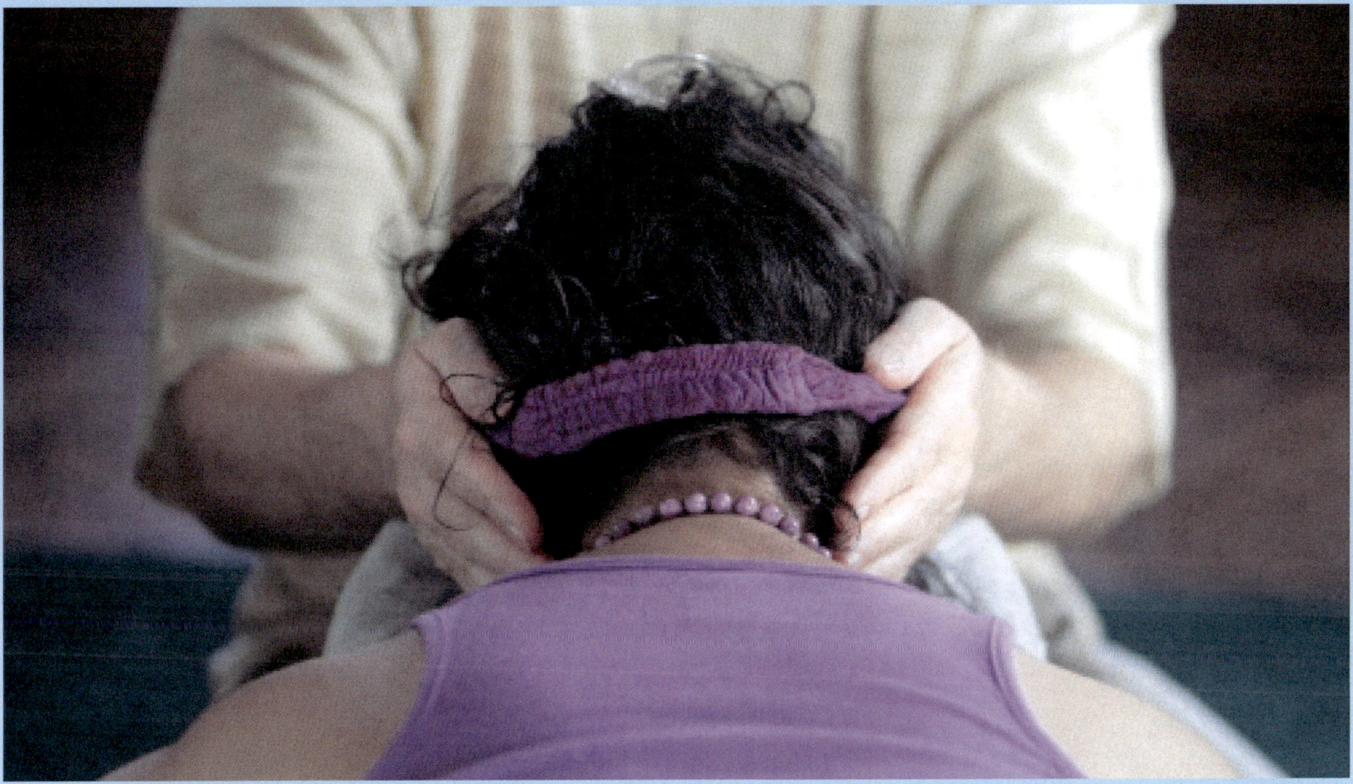

If I've already done a complete healing on the front, I don't usually repeat the head positions, but will do all the back positions starting with the neck.

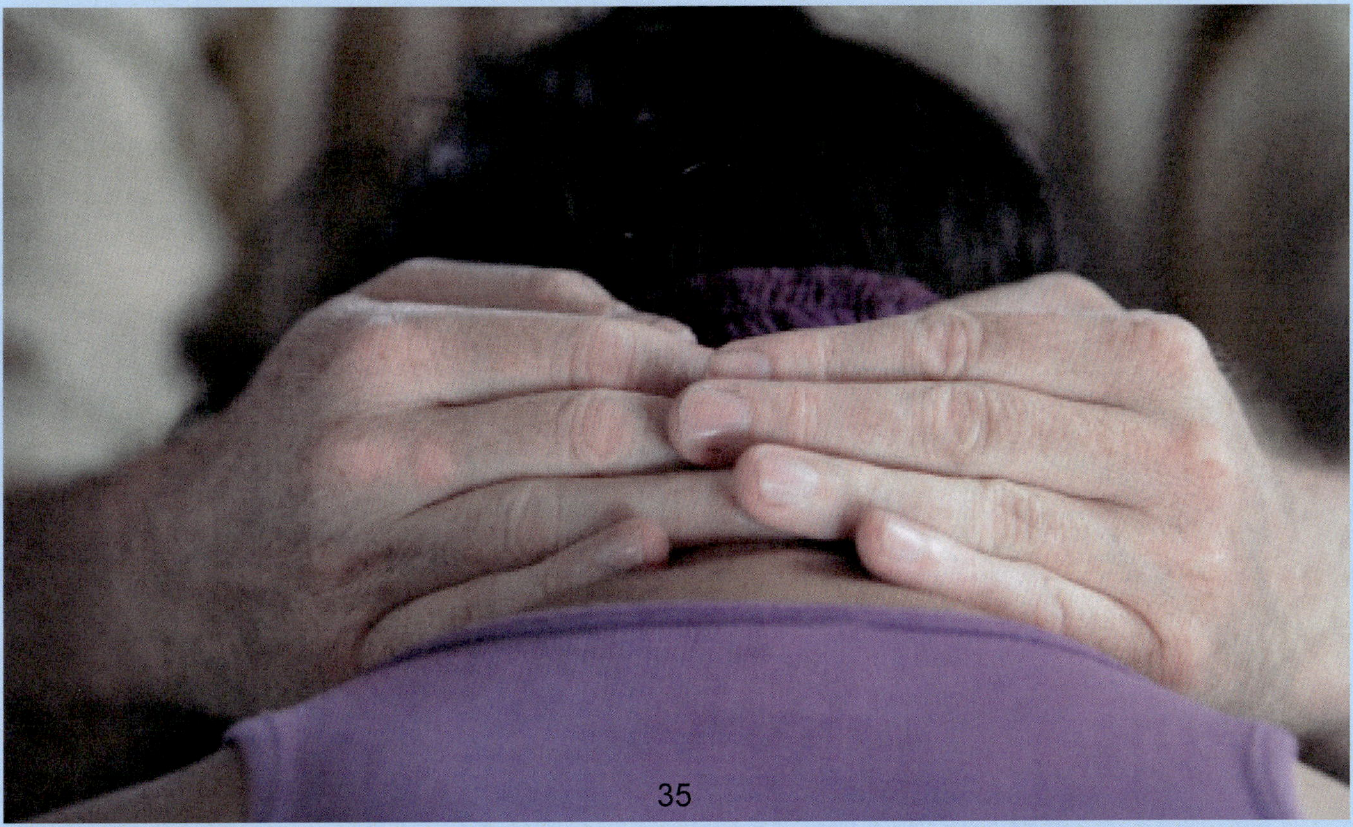

If the client has back problems, especially lower back problems, having them lay face down on the table could add to any strain they already have. In this case, it might be better to treat the back from a seated position.

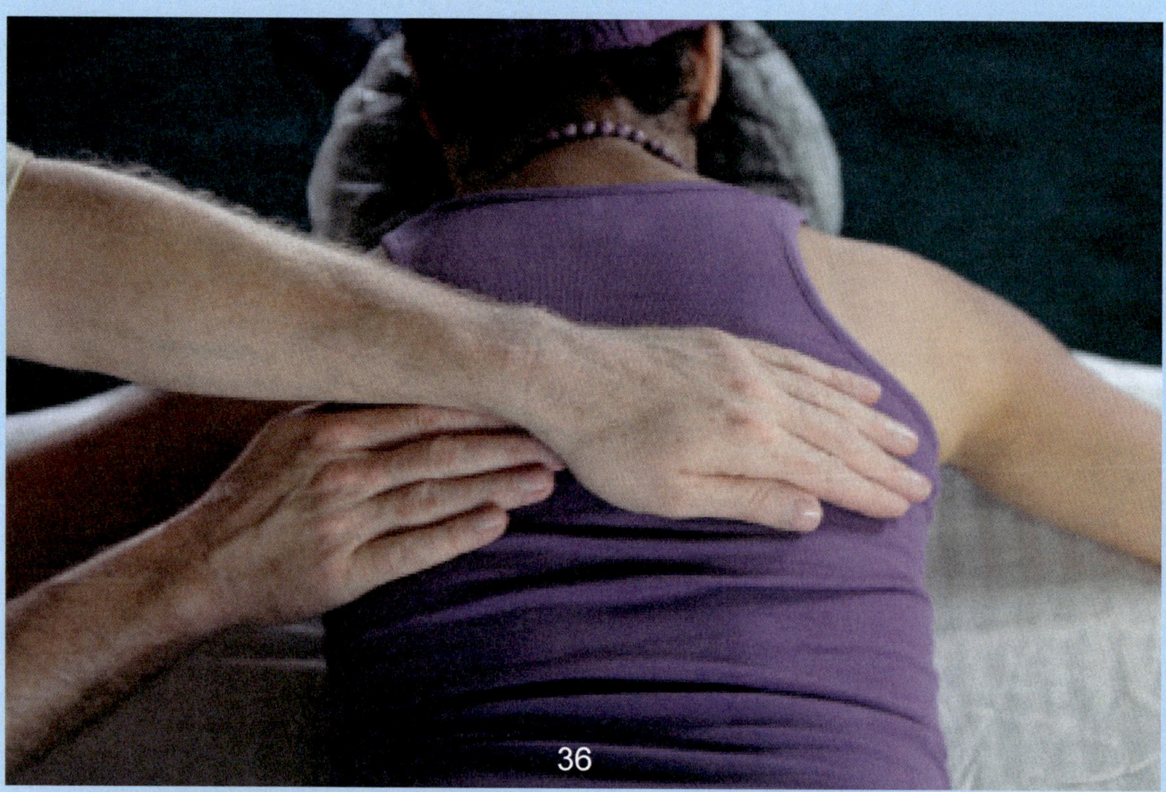

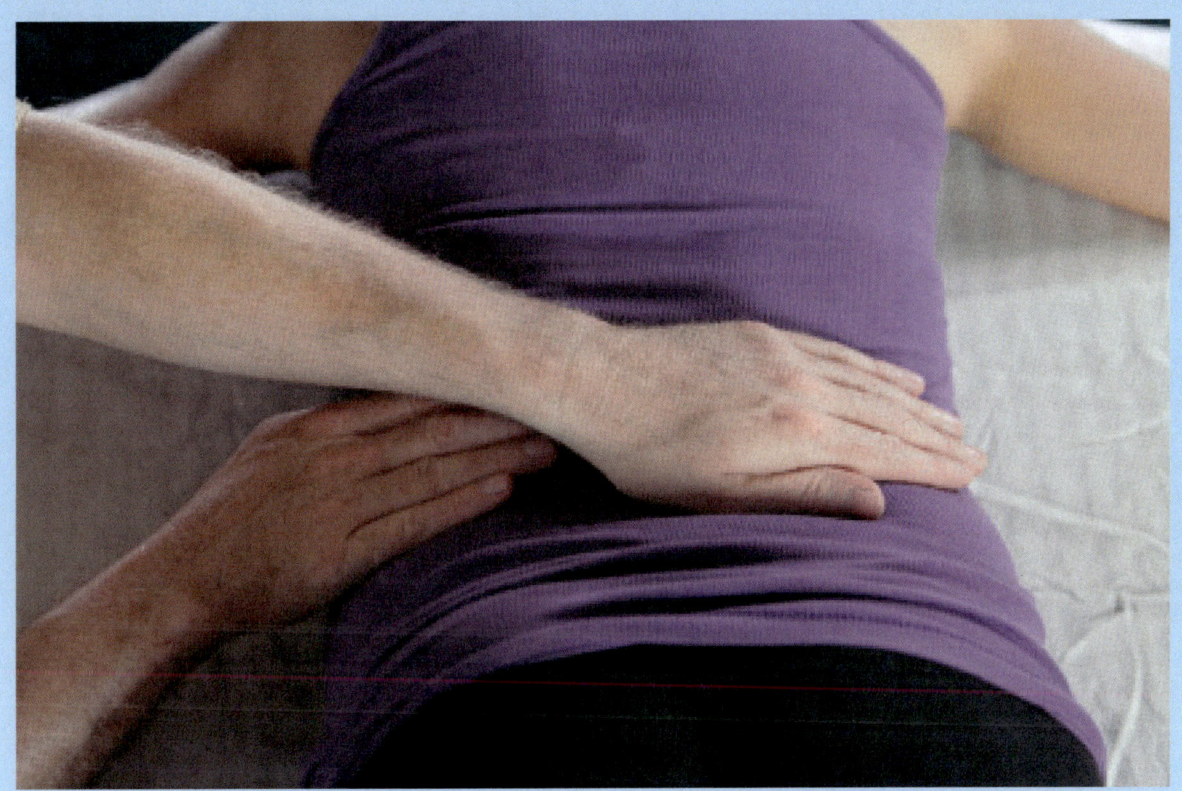

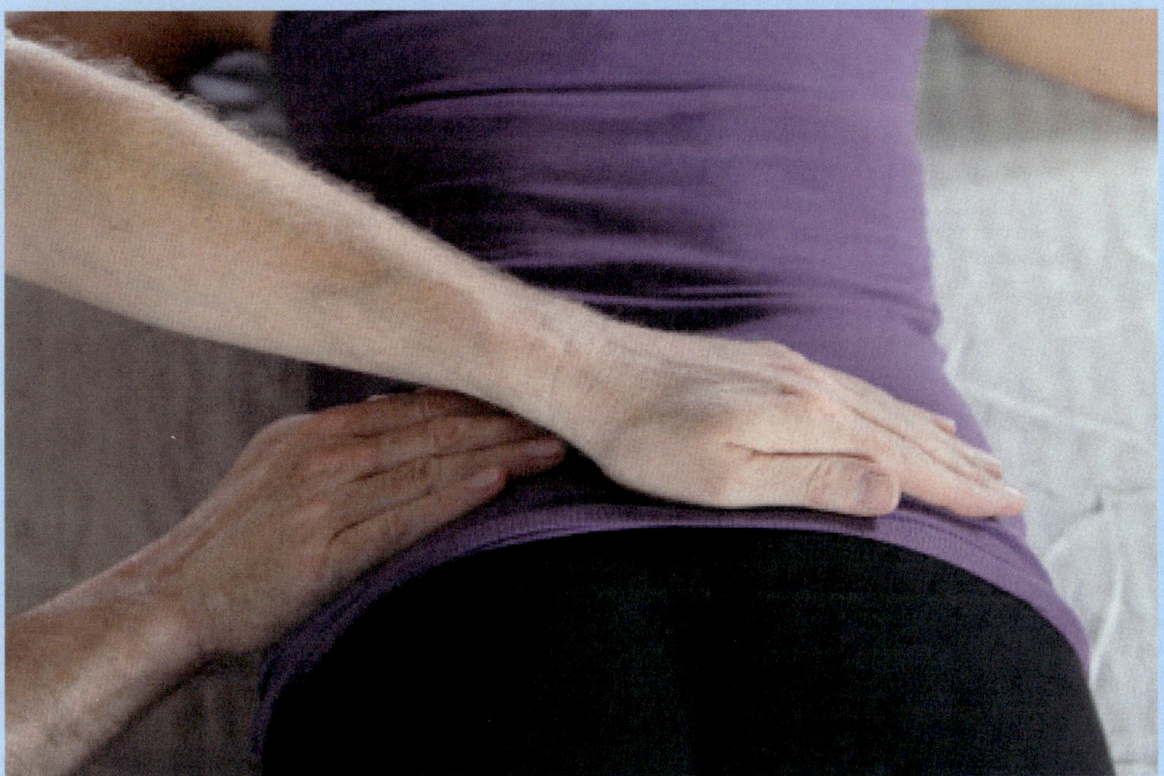

After the lower back (shown here), you can put the hands a few inches above the tailbone to work the root chakra (not pictured).

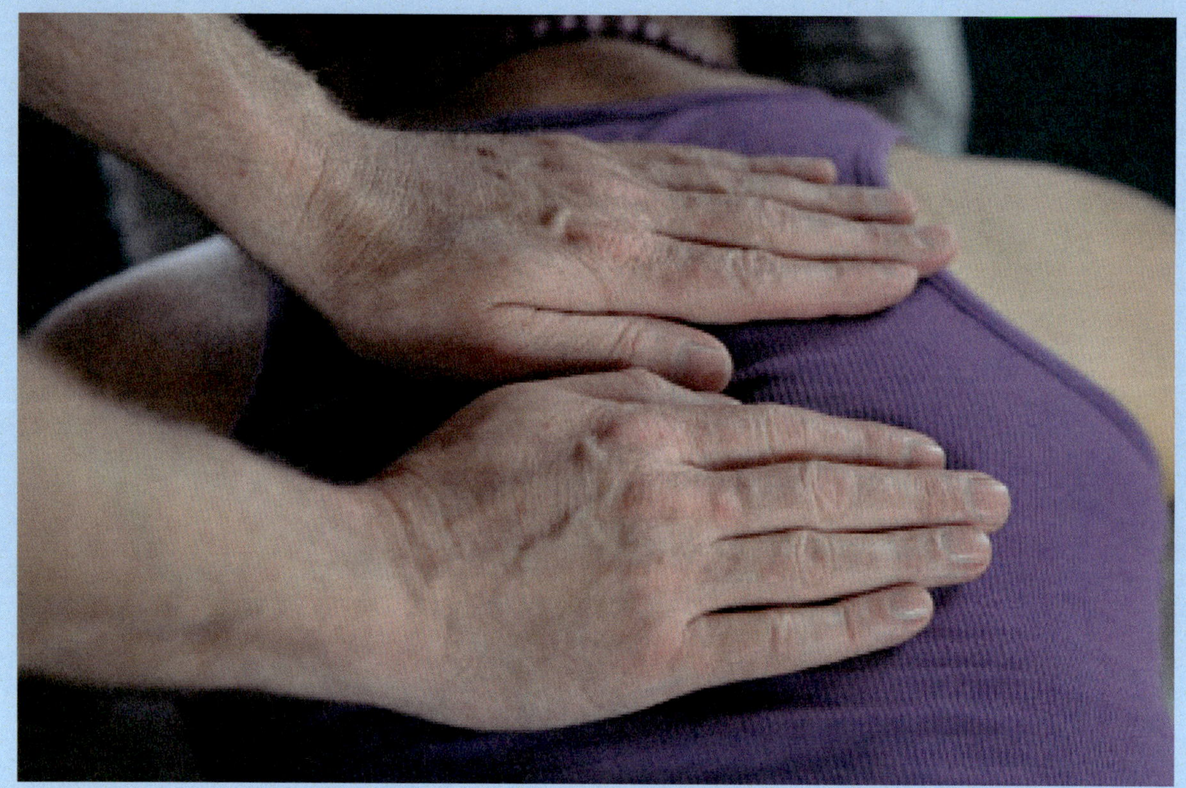

Hands can also be placed side by side or spread out as shown.

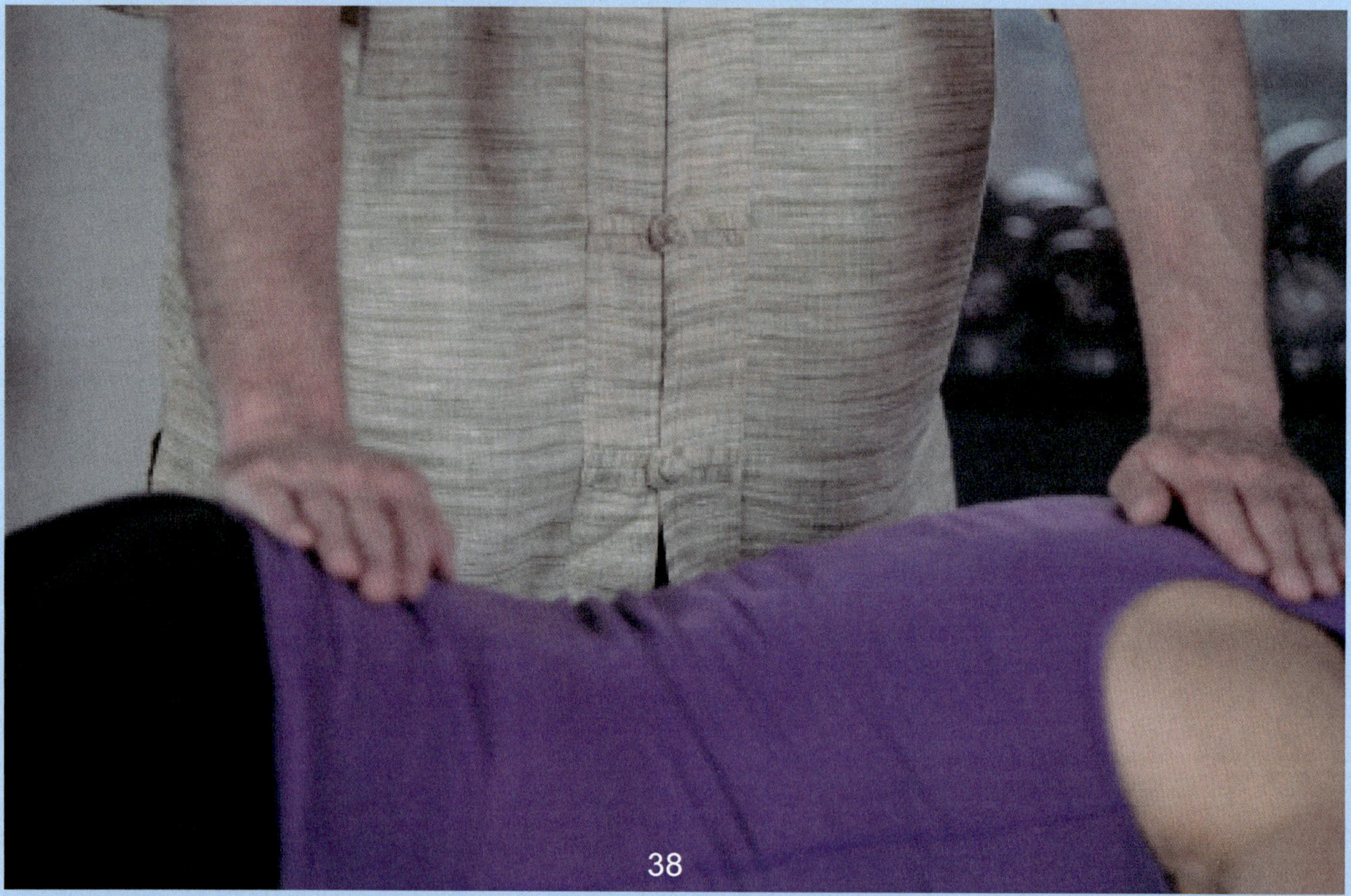

I went to my first Reiki session when I was going through my divorce. I had a friend who mentioned she had a "healer," and in my pain, that sounded like a glass of water after crossing a desert. I had a constant throbbing pain in my right shoulder blade I couldn't seem to lose with ibuprofen, the chiropractor, or doctor's visits. My soul hurt. My body hurt. I was prime for healing.

My Reiki goddess, Rita, sat down with me and discussed everything happening in my life, goals for the session, etc. She then placed me on a massage table and sat down next to me. I had no idea what to expect from a Reiki session so after a few quiet moments when she reached under my shoulder to touch the point that was hurting, I was a bit surprised. She asked me, "What is this?" Out of me bubbled an answer without thought, "betrayal." Throughout the course of that session we dug through layers of betrayal. At first I thought it was my husband's betrayal as he was divorcing me. At quitting us. Then as the session went on it became apparent that it was my own betrayal of self. Desperately clinging to a marriage that did not honor my soul and made me miserable. Not loving myself enough to expect love for myself. Not using my voice because it was punished. Allowing myself to become so NOT myself. The layers of pain simply fell away.

I compare that Reiki session to years of therapy. Effortlessly, I exposed the pain within myself, both hidden and known, and released it. I left Rita not only without an aching shoulder, but with an aura I described at the time as a peppermint, as it was so tingly and joy-filled. The session gave me a center to return to when I got out of whack. It taught me what it is to feel healthy, to be love. I cannot say enough about the powerful transformation that occurred in that session. I was blessed the day I met Rita. I continue to treasure the blessings she provides.
~Andrea D., USA

In December 1998 I had a nasty fall and broke my wrist badly. According to the orthopedic surgeon the damage was so severe I could consider myself disabled as I had lost the use of my wrist almost completely.

Several years later, I became very ill and went to a Reiki Master named Lynda for healing. During the session, I felt my hand being held and then rotated. The pain was excruciating but I breathed through it with tears streaming down my cheeks. This continued for several minutes and included my arm being lifted and the hand being flexed back and forth. I thought Lynda was doing this and since it was my first session I thought it was part of the treatment.

After what I thought was hours, the session finished and I asked Lynda why she had worked so intensely on my hand when I had come for healing on my lungs and thyroid. She had not even been with me when this had happened but had stepped away to re-light her candle. She said that as she turned back toward me she saw what was happening and stood silently by in awe of Spirit working with my hand.

A couple of months later, I had x-rays on my wrist and the doctor was amazed as he stared at them. The damage had been vastly reversed and it was quite apparent that the bones had begun to regenerate.

In time I would have had to have a wrist fusion but because of the Reiki session and subsequent healing I no longer need to have this procedure. I now have approximately 80% flection and rotation in my wrist, as opposed to 10% I had before the session.

This has led me to study Reiki and I am pleased to say, that this year, I have completed my Master's training and am now a Reiki Master myself.
~Amanda N., South Africa

Self-Healing, Seated

Crown

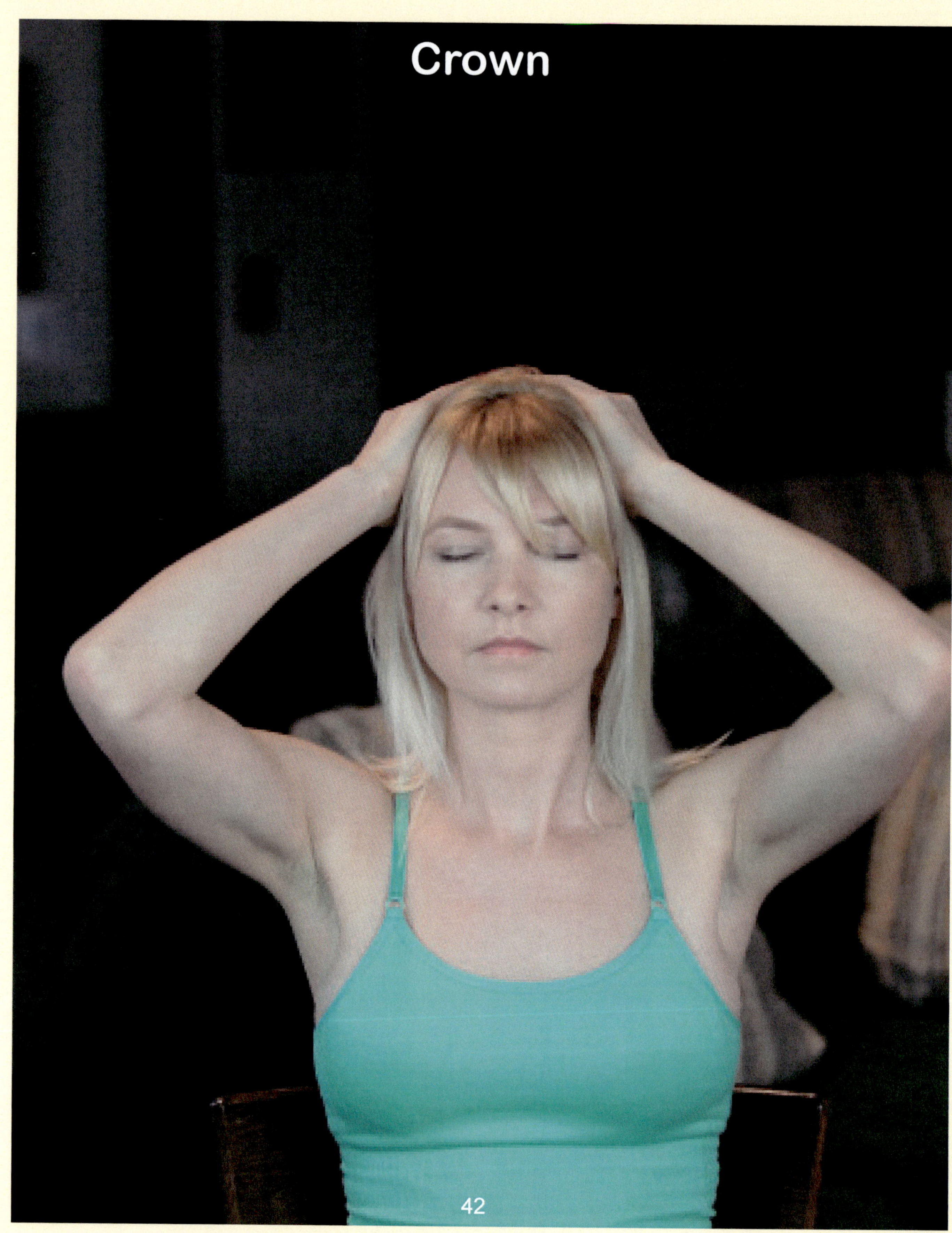

Head/Neck

Optional Position
(Instead of Head/Neck)

Third Eye

My sister found out she had breast cancer 5 yrs ago. I was just getting my 2nd degree level of Reiki as I was sending out healing energy to her. I started to fall deeper and deeper into the healing and I could see where the cancer was. I began to chisel away the cancer spot I saw. When she went back for her second treatment the Dr. said the cancer was gone. She continued with the treatment and she still doesn't believe me when I told her my story but I know the power and healing energy was there for her.
~Denise N., U.S.A.

Throat

Throat, Alternate Position

Heart

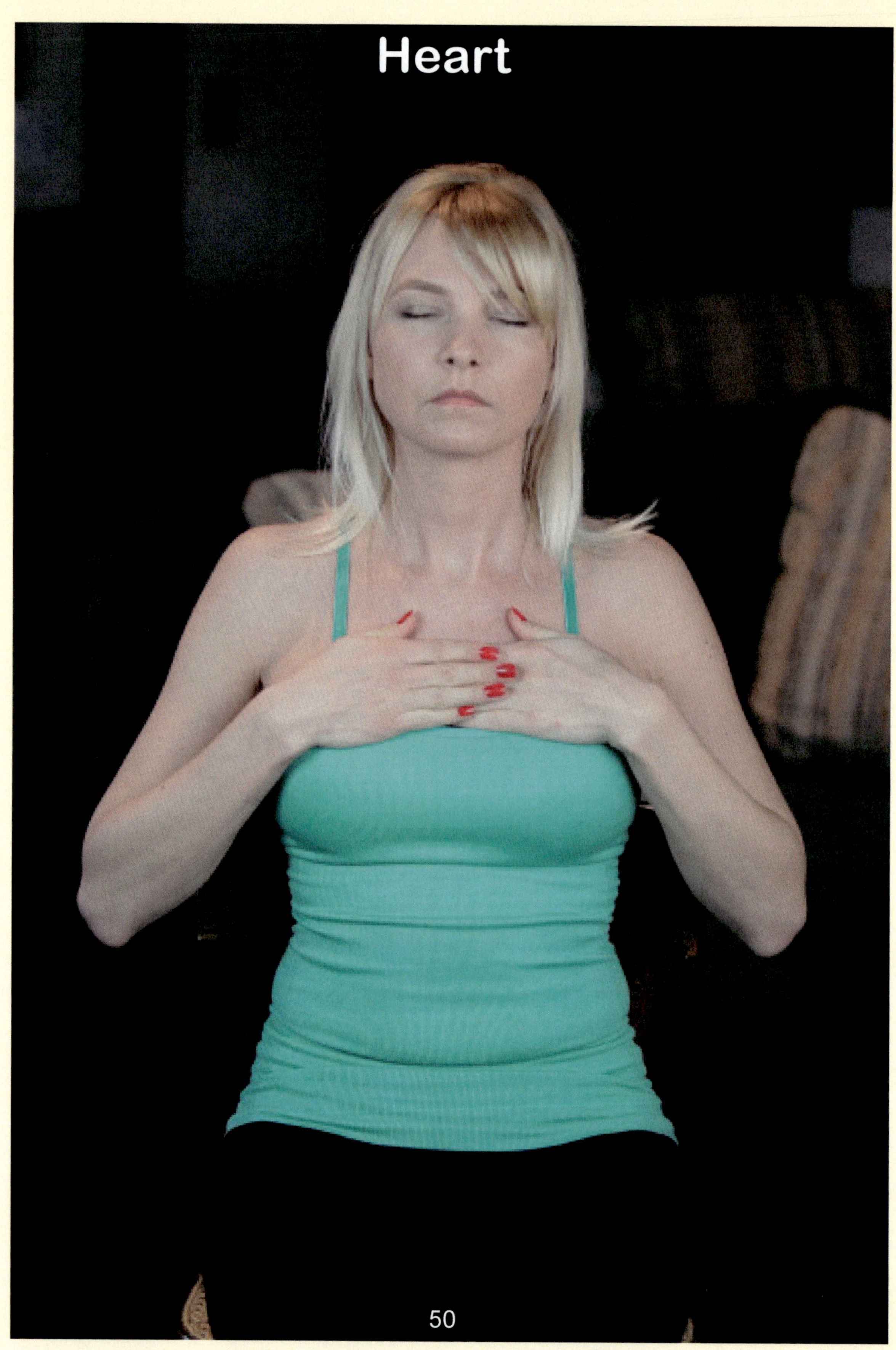

Solar Plexus

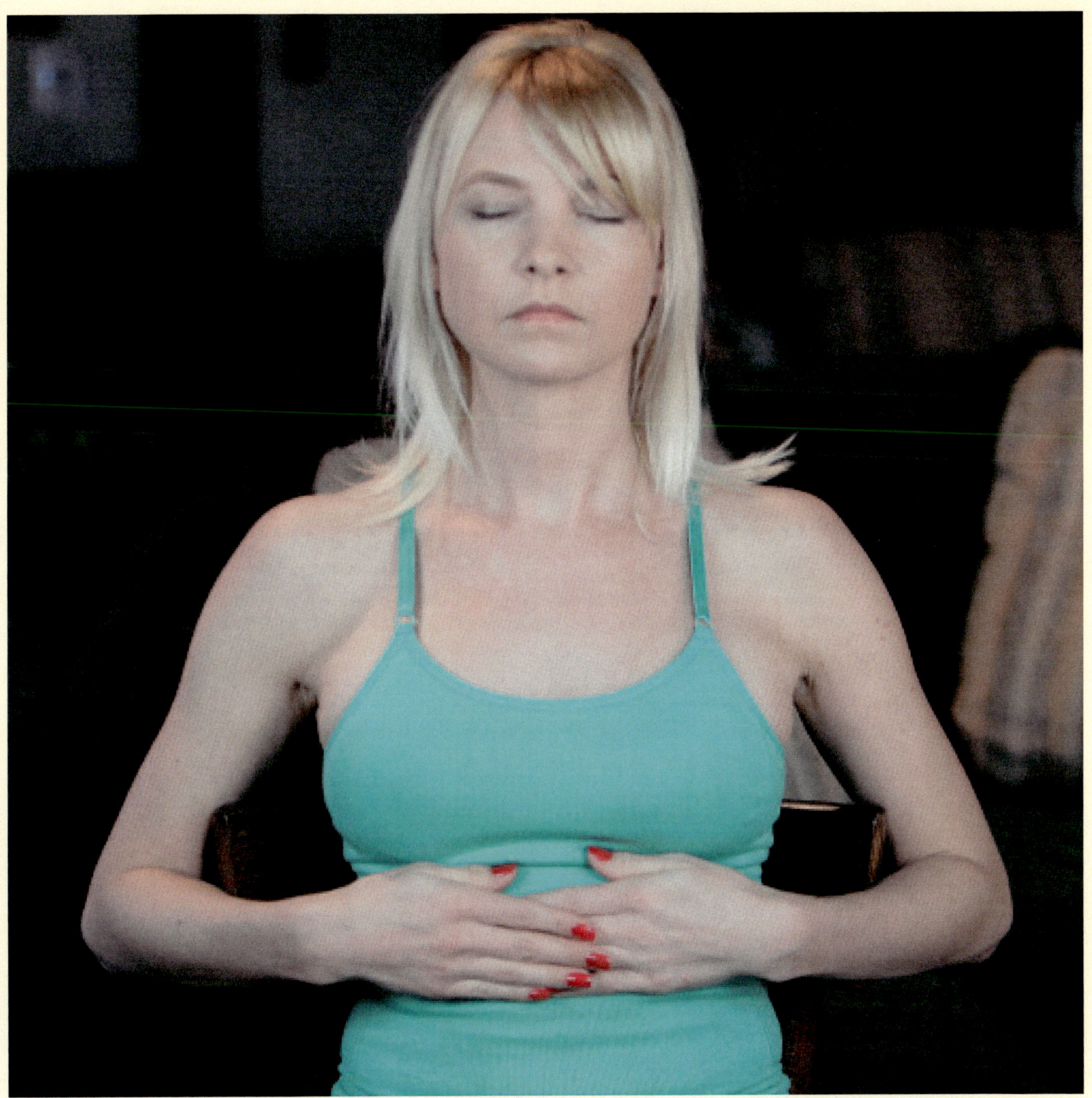

The Solar Plexus is a major power point in the body. It is located just beneath the breasts, or where your ribcage comes together.

The Sacral Plexus is located around the waistline, or just below your navel.

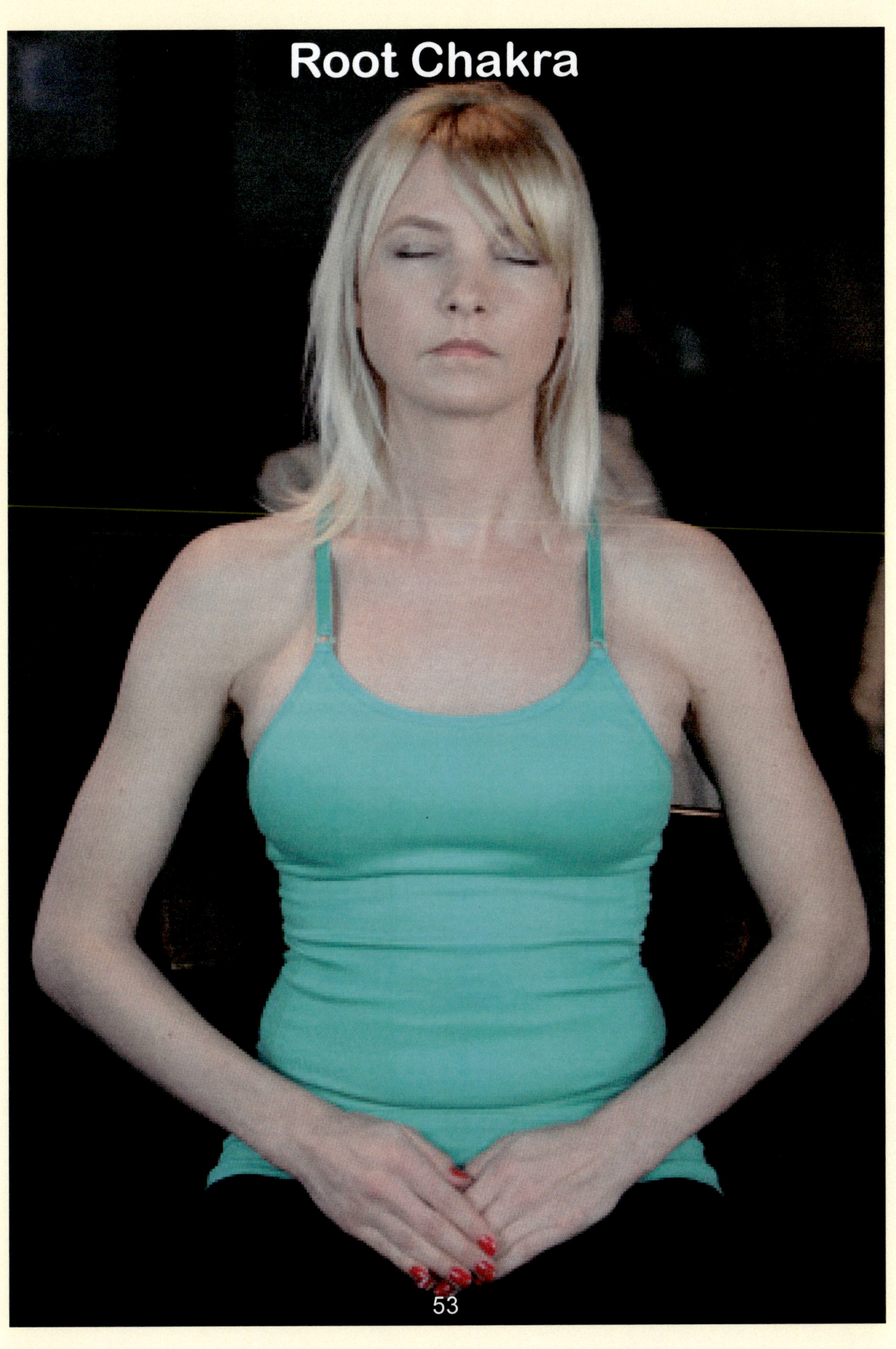
Root Chakra

Knees

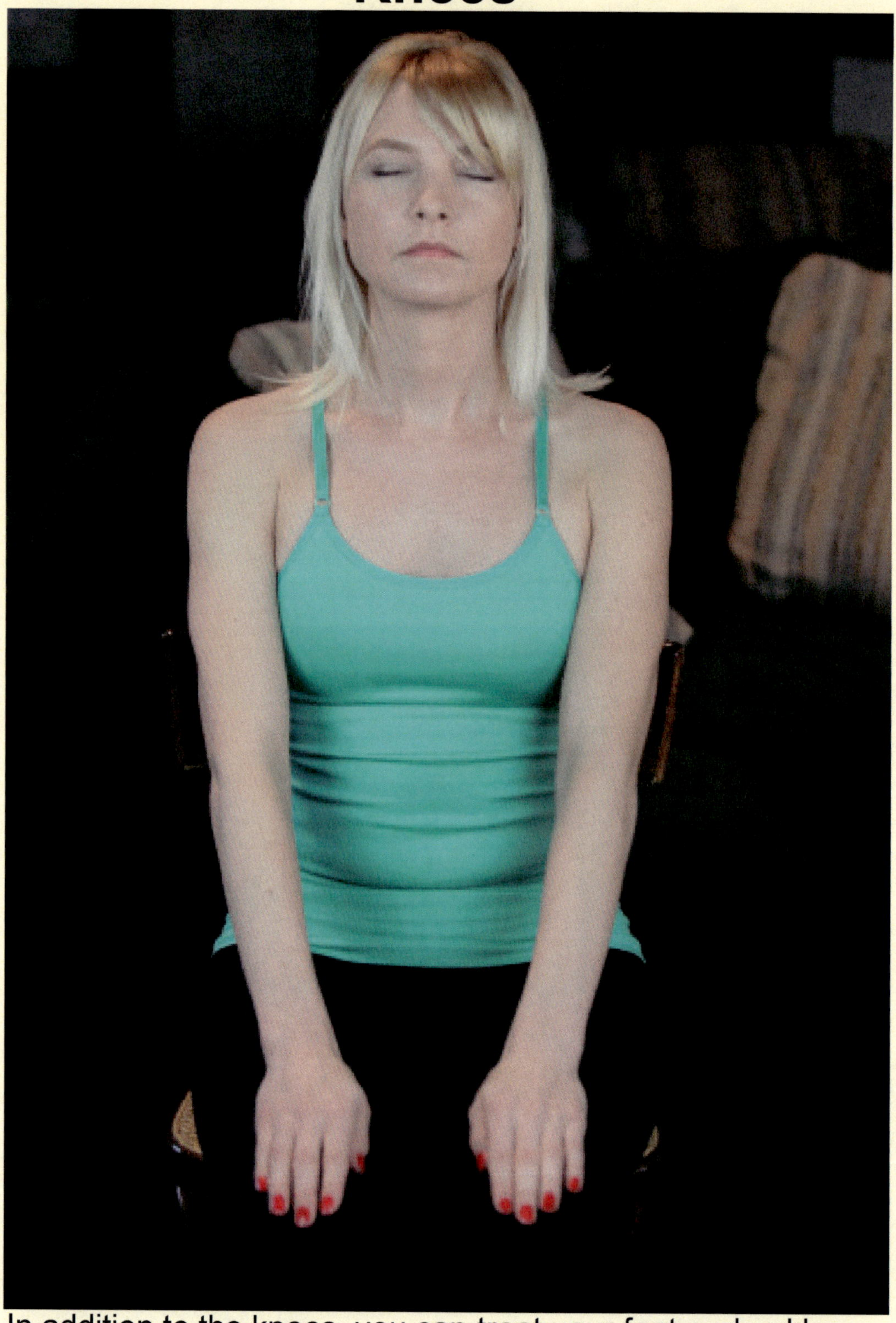

In addition to the knees, you can treat your feet and ankles by placing one hand on the ankle and the other on the soul of each foot (not pictured).

While on a visit to the zoo I was drawn to the gorilla exhibit. A male gorilla was across his pen from me and a child said, "Awe, he looks so sad." My first thought was, "I think I would be too if I lived in a cage after experiencing life in the wild." I stepped up to the the glass enclosure and knocked on the glass. I then put my hands onto the glass and started my healing session. The gorilla came over and sat down right in front of where my hands were placed. I continued to send the energy to him and my hands were quite warm and tingling. A couple of women came up behind me and I heard one say, "I think she is giving him Reiki." After a couple of minutes had passed I removed my hands. I went to leave and the gorilla looked back at me. I stood there and then he knocked on the glass just as I had when I tried to get his attention. I placed my hands back up on the glass.

As facilitators of the healing process we have to remember that our clients come in many different forms. From the person who comes into our place of practice, the tree you come across, a homeless person and any form of life that seeks your help. Whether they are big or small, no matter how insignificant you may think the event may be, treat them all as an amazing opportunity for you to share Reiki with.
Nola P., Canada

I'll admit, when I first joined (your monthly distance healings) I wasn't feeling much of anything. But after several months I'm starting to like the person I see in the mirror and realize what I want and what is toxic in my life. I'm getting the strength to make some much needed big changes and feeling more whole at the same time. It's happening slowly, but I'm noticing some big and wonderful changes in myself, and I really like it. Thank you for your free healings. They are wonderful.
Sara W., USA

I have been always healthy and then suddenly boom, all went wrong. One of the things was a whiplash accident over 7 months ago from which I am still recovering. My life was literally up-side down and there was no way I could go on the three month trip I had planned this winter. I decided to take healing into my own hands and joined your on-line course doing Reiki on myself for three months now. Together with your weekly healing, I am doing better every day. I still have about a third to go but I'm happy to let you know that I'm so much better that I was able to go for one month to Thailand where I am continuing with Reiki intensively.

Thanks a lot for everything.
~Helena K., Switzerland

When I took my first Reiki Class the thing that stuck with me the most was my Reiki teacher saying that anything is available to Reiki. Hands on, Reiki on. She then proceeded to tell us the story of the dying plant that she did Reiki on every day and how it perked up a little each day until it was healthy and thriving. I kept this image in my head, and still do to this day.

Several months after I finished this class and received my Reiki I certificate my dog was hit by a car. We took him to the emergency vet and his right hip was shattered. To get the hip fixed would have cost several thousands of dollars, but being a single mom I was in no position to afford that. I asked the vet what would happen if the hip wasn't surgically repaired and his reply was "well he's got three good legs."

We had to carry this dog out to do his business until eventually, he could walk on three legs and get around on his own. Every day he would lie on the floor next to the couch and I would put my hands on his hip. Slowly, eventually he was able to walk on all four legs again, and even play fetch in the back yard like he used to.

To me it was a defining time in my Reiki learning. It showed me that all are benefieted from this wonderful practice, and what my Reiki Master had taught me was powerfully true---Hands on, Reiki on.
~Lisa M., USA

Healing Others, Seated

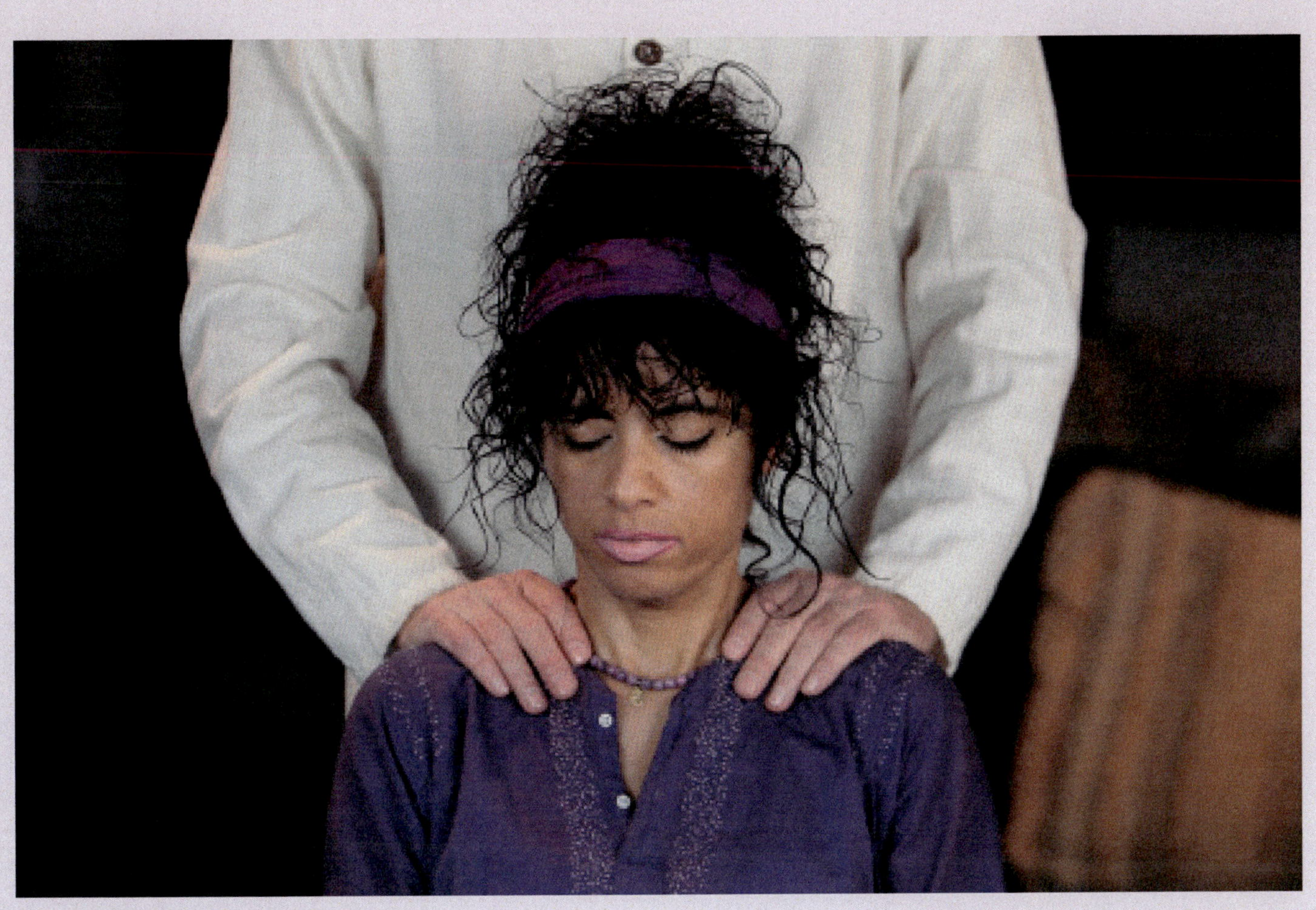

Crown

In this instance, the client is wearing her hair up in a bun. Notice how I've adjusted to acommodate. It is perfectly acceptable to adjust to your hand positions as needed.

Third Eye

Throat

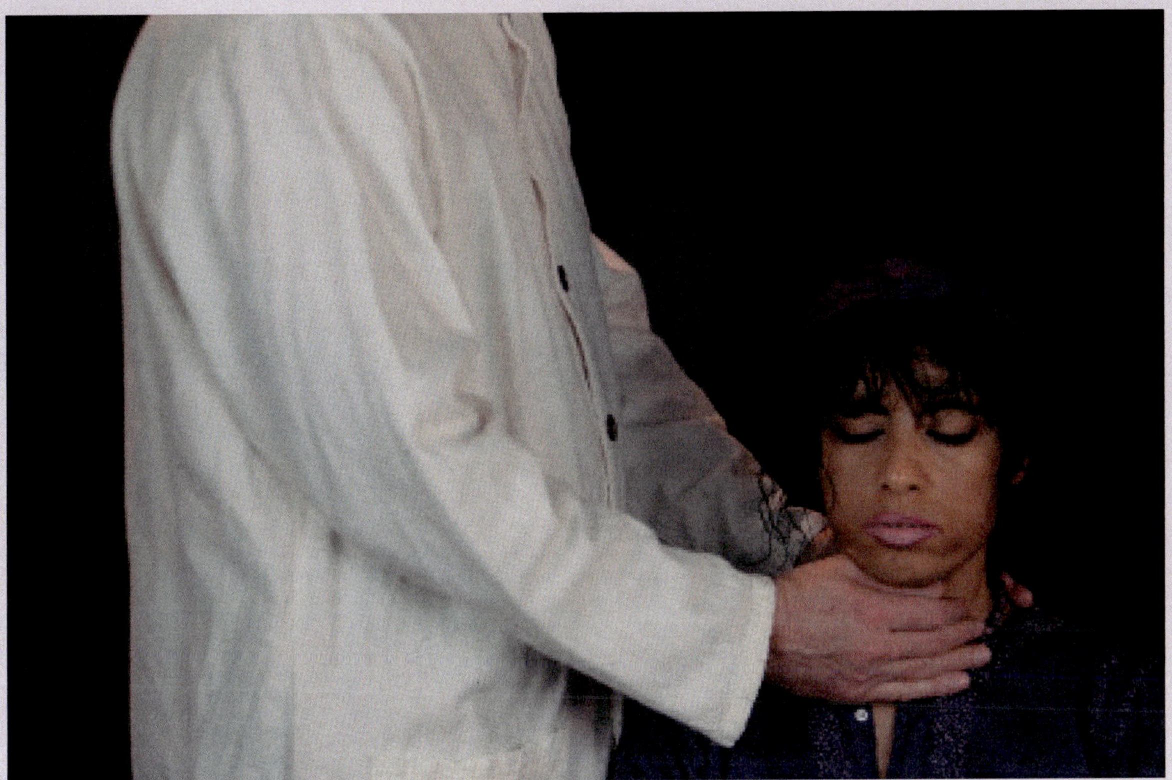

The throat position can be performed from the front or the side, whichever is more comfortable for both the client and the practitioner. Note...a VERY LIGHT TOUCH is necessary so the client doesn't feel like they're being choked.

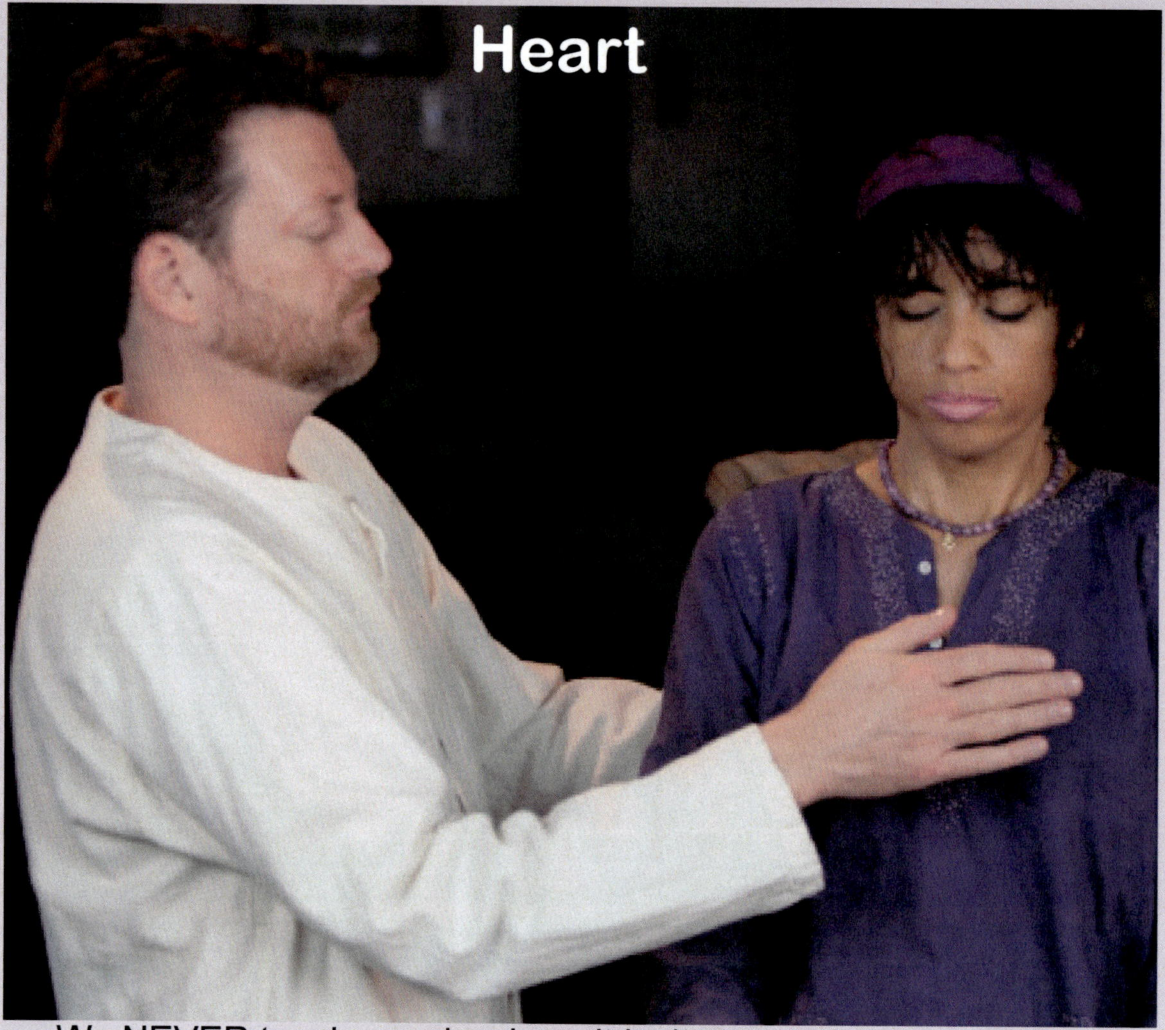

Heart

We NEVER touch people where it isn't appropriate to touch.

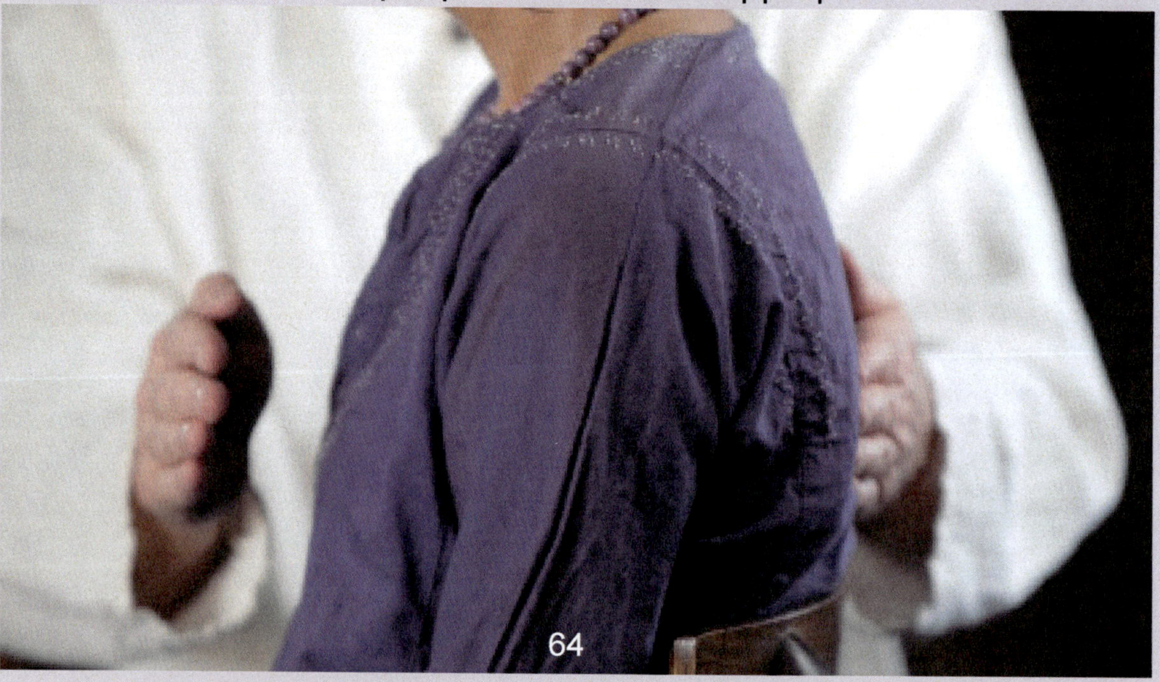

Solar Plexus

Notice my hand is on the back of the chair. It is not necessary to move the client out of position...the energy will pass right through the chair.

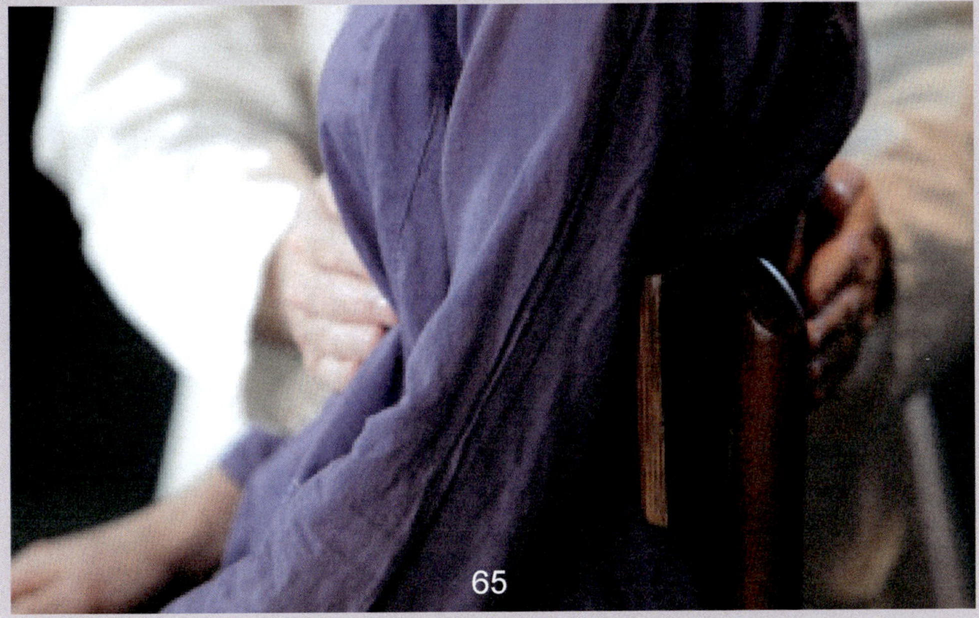

Sacral Plexus

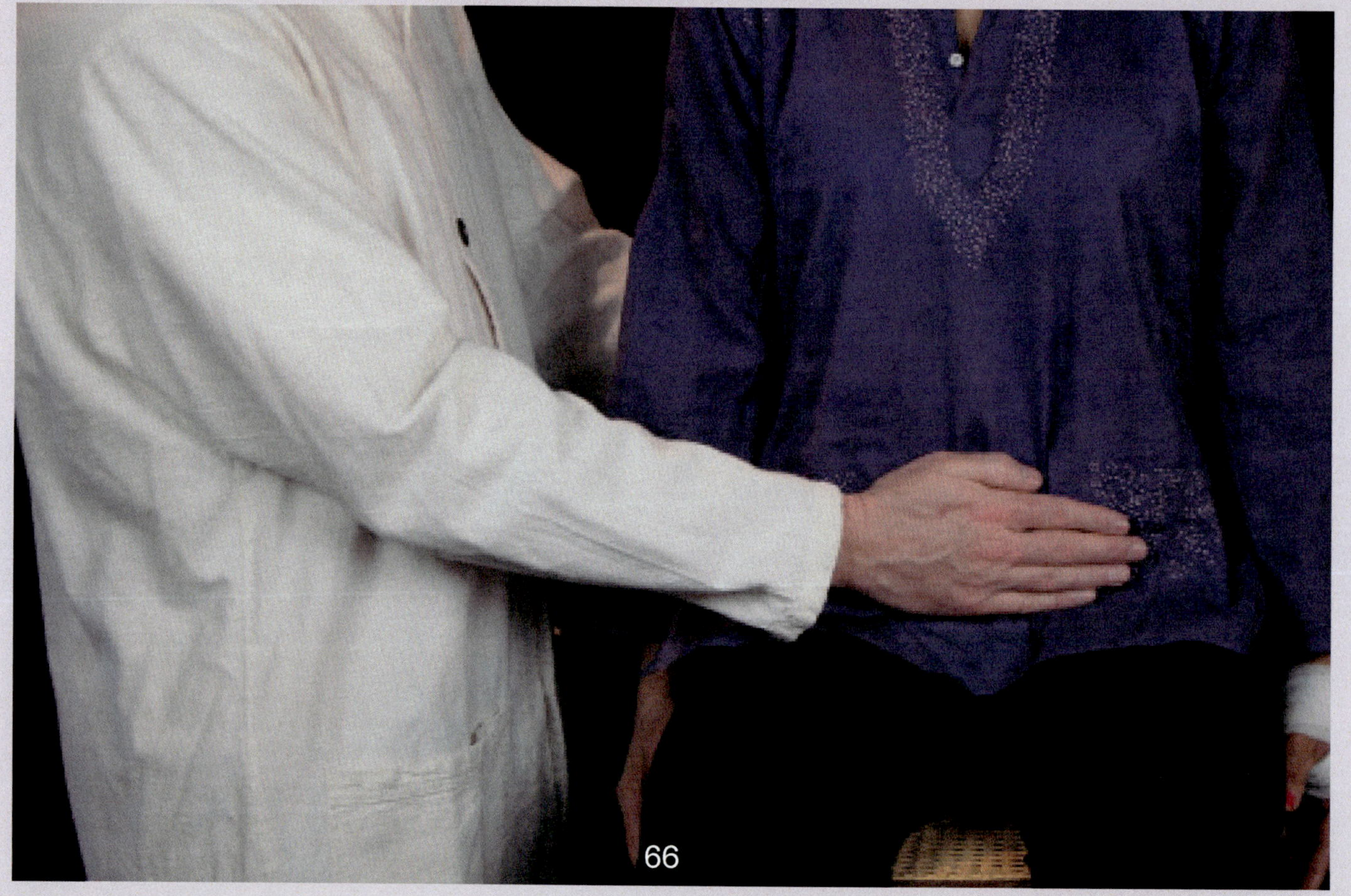

Root

One hand on the lower back, the other hand over the genitalia...again NOT Touching

Knees

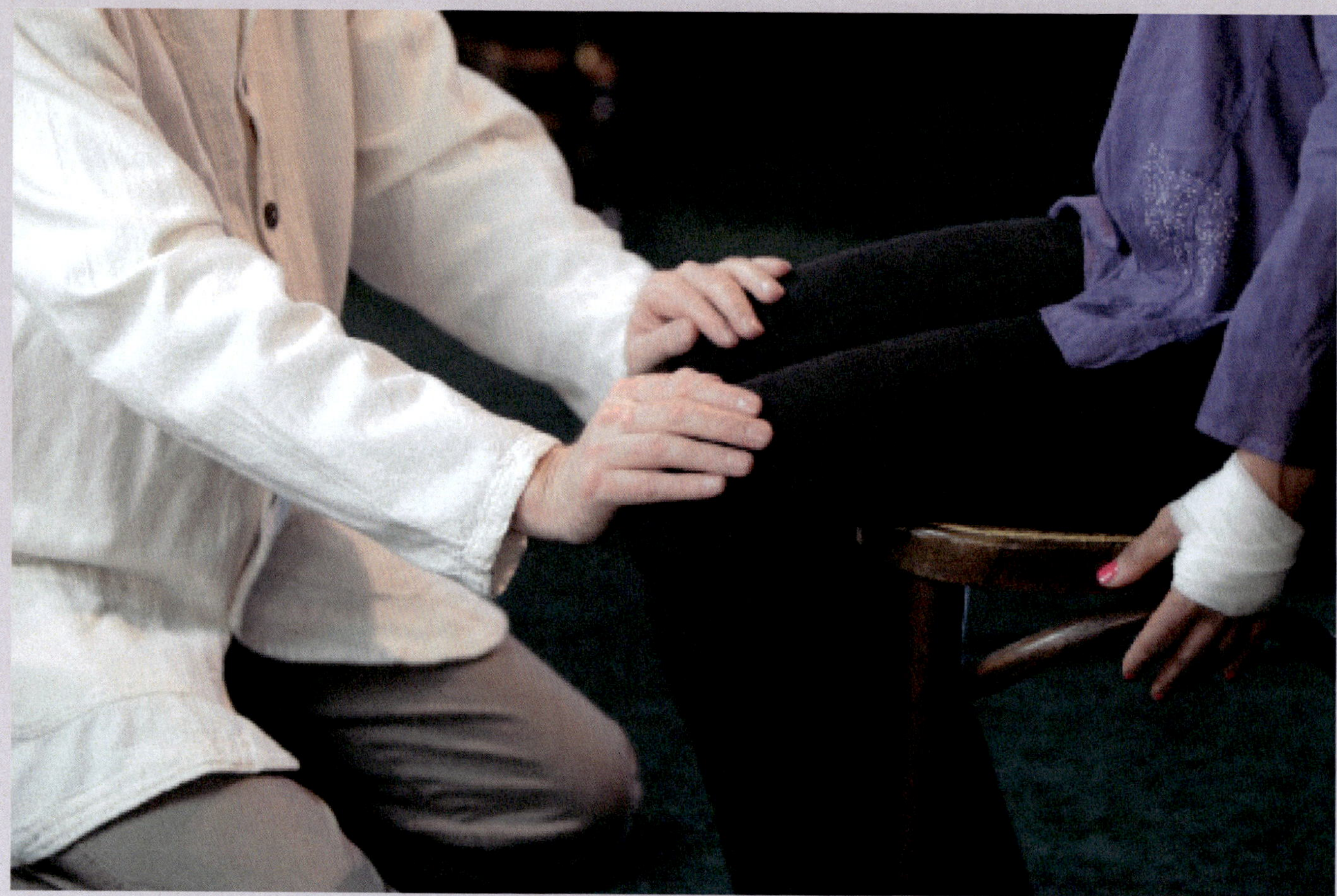

My 11 year old daughter completed Reiki 1 and will be doing Reiki 2 very soon. For a child of her age in primary school she was a nervous wreck when it came to tests, and challenges. On the morning of a test, no matter how well she learned her stuff, she would be nearly sick and crying at the thought of it, and more often than not, have blank moments. With being like this in primary school, I worried how bad she might become in secondary school. She completed Reiki 1 and it has changed her life so much. It has helped her tremendously with her nerves and school tests, as well as her confidence! She's a new person. It's great! She is so eager to complete Reiki 2 now so she can help others. Reiki has changed both our lives in such a positive way!
~Nicola H., Ireland

Feet & Ankles

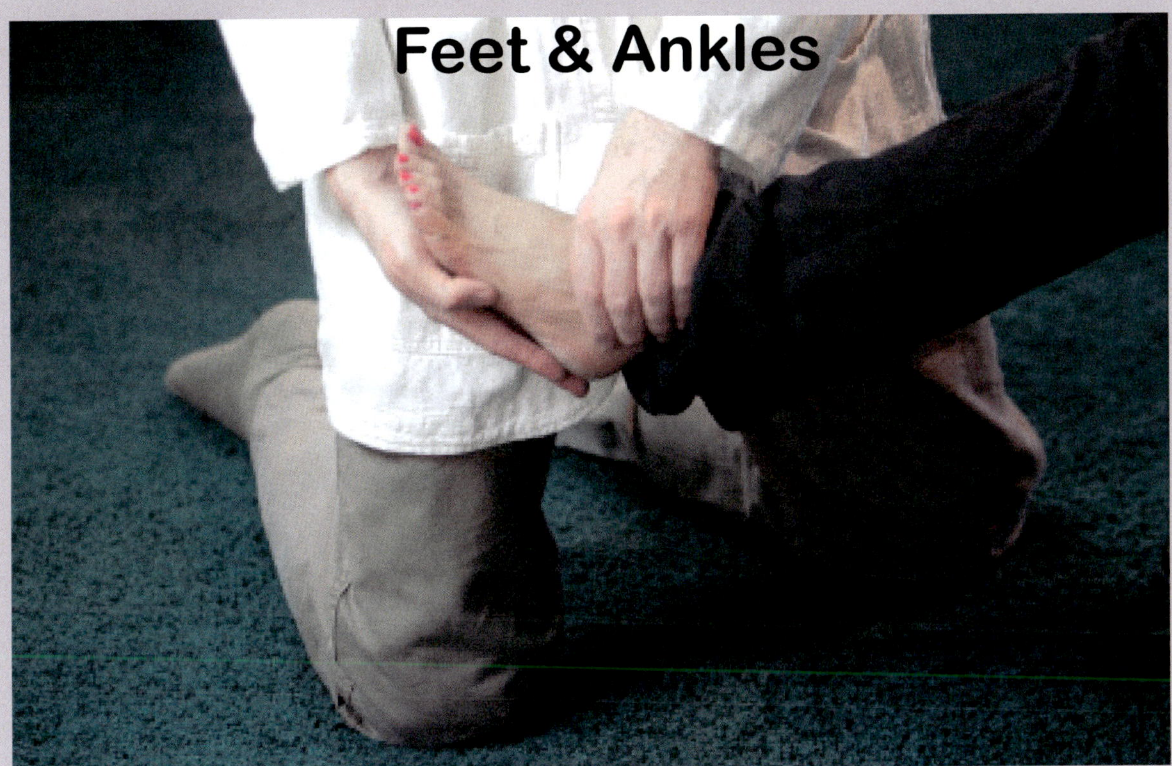

The feet and ankles are often overlooked in treatment. Our ankles can carry a lot of stress. Giving Reiki to the bottoms of the feet can be like an entire reflexology treatment. Ideally shoes come off, but it isn't necessary. There may be situations where the shoes cannot be removed...the energy will pass through the shoes.

Dear Jeff,
You did my attunement in February of 2013. I have been doing Reiki on myself daily and studying a lot about developing my intuition and spiritual healing. When I ordered your course, I was smoking 2 packs of cigarettes a day and I was drinking every night, trying to relieve my problems. I used to get angry and upset over stupid things. My husband has alzheimer's and is very forgetful. I used to get so mad and fight with him all the time because he would forget things. I also worried all the time about money issues. Since doing Reiki on myself every day for six months, I have a whole new outlook on life. I have quit drinking and smoking. I have learned how to deal with my feelings and to accept them for what they are. I have more understanding for my husband's condition and no longer fight with him. Since I quit worring about money and changed my mental outlook, my massage business has really picked up. I no longer worry about how I am going to pay my bills. Learning Reiki has totally transformed my life physically, mentally, and emotionally. I am so blessed now. I am so glad that I took your course in Reiki and am so excited to learn more. I am a new person now and on a new path on spiritual healing so I will be able to help my clients more. God bless you.
~Jennifer M., USA

I found a hard lump at the base of my throat and had my doctor do an ultrasound. They found a 3 cm cold nodule. I was having biopsies every six months to rule out malignancy. The endocrinologist recommended surgery, so I went to see a surgeon. I asked if I could do something to get rid of the lump, but I was told surgery was the only way! I declined and asked for a little more time as surgery was too invasive. I didn't want my thyroid removed because of a nodule!! I started doing self Reiki, tai chi, & meditation. After three months the biopsy revealed no nodule. My doctor sent me immediately to the lab for yet another biopsy, but this time done by a doctor. He also couldn't find a nodule. I told the endocrinologist what I had done, but he said it was not possible, yet he had no explanation. He was baffled, I was ecstatic!!! To this day my doctor has no answer, other than it has shifted to another location. This was a hard lump I found, it could not be moved manually, so I'm positive it didn't go anywhere, but away.
~Antoinette S., Canada

About the Author

I've been a student of metaphysics and energy since 1993. In 2001, I took workshops in the the first two levels of Reiki and quickly began seeing results. In early 2003, I awoke one night with the knowing, the urging that I had to become a Reiki Master. The same thing happened the next night and the next night. Finally, after 10 sleepless nights, I took my Master training and from there, my life took a quantum leap.

It seems the Universe was serious, because the very day I took my Master's course, I stopped to visit a chiropractor friend of mine, told him what I had done and he offered to share his office with me. Within weeks I started hosting free Reiki intro nights and began teaching, with the belief that for every person I taught, many more would feel touched by this incredible healing energy.

Reiki has completely changed my life. With all humility, I can honestly say Reiki has made me a kinder, gentler person. It has also propelled me on a spiritual path I never imagined. Doors have opened I never knew existed. I've seen miraculous healings on physical, spiritual and emotional levels.

My hope is that Reiki touches your life the way it has touched mine.

Many Blessings,

Jeff

For more information on Jeff, his healings and teachings, go to **www.HomeStudyReiki.com**

The Reiki Principles

- Just for today, I will not anger.
- Just for today, I will not worry.
- Just for today, I will give thanks for my many blessings.
- Just for today, I will do my work honestly.
- Just for today, I will be kind to my neighbor and every living thing.

~Mikao Usui

Made in the USA
Middletown, DE
19 June 2017